BERKLEE PRESS

EXPLORING
CLASSICAL
MANDOLIN

TECHNIQUE & REPERTOIRE

To access audio and video visit:
www.halleonard.com/mylibrary

Enter Code
8816-7916-0996-5443

AUGUST WATTERS

Berklee Press

Editor in Chief: Jonathan Feist
Vice President of Online Learning and Continuing Education/CEO of Berklee Online: Debbie Cavalier
Assistant Vice President of Marketing and Recruitment for Berklee Media: Mike King
Dean of Continuing Education: Carin Nuernberg
Editorial Assistants: Emily Jones, Eloise Kelsey
Illustrator: Anna Welch
Author Photo: Robert Patton
Video Producer: A J Dimaculangan
Audio Engineer: Robert Patton

ISBN 978-0-87639-162-4

1140 Boylston Street
Boston, MA 02215-3693 USA
(617) 747-2146

Visit Berklee Press Online at
www.berkleepress.com

Study with

■ **BERKLEE ONLINE**

online.berklee.edu

DISTRIBUTED BY

HAL•LEONARD®
CORPORATION
7777 W. BLUEMOUND RD. P.O. BOX 13819
MILWAUKEE, WISCONSIN 53213

Visit Hal Leonard Online at
www.halleonard.com

Berklee Press, a publishing activity of Berklee College of Music, is a not-for-profit educational publisher.
Available proceeds from the sales of our products are contributed to the scholarship funds of the college.

CONTENTS

ACKNOWLEDGMENTS

I have been fortunate, in my own music studies, to have been guided by some of the most accomplished classical mandolinists on the scene today, and by other knowledgeable and specialized musicians. My most influential mentors and colleagues have been endlessly generous with their time and knowledge. Many thanks to:

- Emanuele Cappellotto, for sharing his vast knowledge of the Italian mandolin, its history, pedagogy, and current practice

- Annika Hinsche, for her enthusiastic help to understand the mandolin's place in the German educational system, as well as her deep understanding of our instrument's classical traditions

- Ugo Orlandi, for his hospitality, insight, and wisdom

- Carlo Aonzo, for his tireless advocacy for the mandolin, and his equally tireless patience as a teacher and role model. And did I mention his peerless technique?

- Marilynn Mair, "First Lady of the American Mandolin," for her generosity, impeccable musicianship, encyclopedic knowledge, and endless curiosity

- Bob Harrigan, who first lead me to the chord/melody concept that would later guide my learning on mandolin

- William G. Leavitt, who demonstrated a deep sensitivity to his students and the creativity to compose didactic yet thoroughly musical and satisfying etudes to address their needs

- David N. Baker, for his literate, sophisticated, and soulful approach to understanding and teaching America's music

- Vona L. Davis, who taught me respect and curiosity for American music in all its forms, and showed me the way toward a lifelong path of musical study

Additional thanks to the following: Mark Davis, Mark Levesque, Joe Thomas, Alex Timmerman, Ted Mann, Robert A. Margo, and Anna Welch. I couldn't have done it without you!

And above all to my wife Nancy, without whom (in so many ways) none of this would have been possible.

INTRODUCTION

It's an exciting time to be a mandolinist! Ideas flow across old musical boundaries, enabling new ways of being creative. Internet communication creates a platform for new learning styles and offers access to a trove of information, much of which had previously been lost or inaccessible. In today's musical environment, creative musicians can easily borrow from whatever sources they most enjoy and synthesize their own creative points of view.

There is always another way of seeing things, of course. Internet culture also makes it easy to skim across the surface of deep traditions, overlooking critical context and diminishing the perceived value of expertise. The types of learning enabled by the Internet may or may not effectively showcase what those traditions have to offer, and the wisdom of the ages—represented in the best works of previous generations—may not even be available on the web. In this environment, it can be difficult to tell what has influenced our development, or for that matter, why we should care!

Classical mandolin—even though it formed the beginnings of mandolin music in America—is easy to overlook. Mandolinists are often unfamiliar with America's first popular mandolin style, the classical mandolin, and how it contributed to today's stylistic and technical trends. No study of American mandolin styles is complete without the music that started it all: classical mandolin.

Exploring Classical Mandolin is designed as a practical resource for the contemporary mandolinist. Above all, this book seeks to answer the question: "What does classical mandolin have to offer to the practicing mandolinist from a different background?" With careful study, this book will:

- illuminate approaches to technique and tone production rooted in our own instrumental traditions, and going beyond today's common practice

- highlight exciting and little-explored avenues for future exploration

- help you express your own ideas for arranging, composing, and improvising within classical mandolin and related traditions

- illustrate the connections between classical mandolin and other approaches

- clarify the difference between music composed and arranged for classical mandolin

- connect to the various traditions of classical mandolin, for further study

Exploring Classical Mandolin is not designed as an alternative to the study of classical mandolin through one of its existing national traditions; quite the opposite! My hope is that this book will be a starting point for learning what each of these traditions—such as those from Italy, France, the United States, Germany, and Japan—has to offer. I also hope that musicians who have studied within one or more of these traditions will find in this book an international perspective, as well as valuable information on connecting to the broader traditions of our instrument—such as arranging, chord-melody playing, and improvisation—that are underrepresented in today's mandolin educational system.

I'm excited to be able to highlight some possibilities for exploring new paths on the mandolin while connecting the study of the modern mandolin to its deep traditions. For American mandolinists, I hope this book will provide critical context for serious study of our versatile instrument. Classical music is not peripheral to the American mandolin; it's the "big bang" that started it all! Every student of the American mandolin should have an opportunity to explore how America's first popular mandolin style gradually entwined with ragtime, barbershop, string band music, and the blues—decades before bluegrass music was created. I hope that for today's practicing mandolinists, connecting to these musical roots—and extending them into today's music—will provide endless, joyful hours of exploration.

Classical mandolin is a living tradition. It offers different ways of thinking about technique and tone, and opportunities to explore all the colors and moods of our versatile (and often misunderstood) instrument.

HOW TO USE THIS BOOK

This book is divided into three parts: practice method, classical mandolin repertoire, and arrangements of classical music not originally written for mandolin. Part I contains conceptual materials, as well as etudes, for practicing and developing those ideas. Parts II and III are more oriented toward concert music. Together, the three sections present what I have found to be the most effective technical and conceptual approaches, based on many years teaching hundreds of students.

If you are ready to dive into the music, please go directly to the beginning of part II, a brief overview of classical music composed for mandolin. There, you will find cornerstones of the classical mandolin repertoire, as well as lesser-known works chosen to represent important styles and eras of mandolin music. The easier works are toward the beginning, and the only skills assumed there are a basic level of instrumental technique plus the ability to read standard notation.

As you work through part II, you will probably discover that the works gradually become more difficult. If you find yourself spending hours memorizing fingerings, or staring at your left hand to find the notes, it's probably time to delve into part I—a practice approach for contemporary classical mandolin. Part I targets the specific skills you need, and develops in a systematic way. I have made references in the footnotes throughout to other methods (mostly in the public domain) for further practice.[1]

Part III contains classical music arranged for solo mandolin. There are arrangements from other composers (since arranging music from other instruments to mandolin is an old tradition!), but most of the works in part III are my own arrangements of familiar classical melodies. Like part II, part III is arranged with easiest pieces first. As they develop, both

---

[1] My first recommendation: if you need help with standard notation, I recommend the *Hal Leonard Mandolin Method Book 1*, by Rich DelGrosso. This book begins with tablature, and teaches standard notation using popular American folk tunes.

part II and part III use some of the more challenging material from part I, chapters 4 and 5. Part II ends with my own compositions, employing contemporary techniques and harmonic language as presented in part I, chapters 5 and 6.

I do not recommend spending too much time learning by rote memorization; it's usually better to target the underlying skills needed to play a new piece. Perhaps the most valuable contribution this book can make is to help you develop a regular practice routine that amplifies your learning experience. As you approach a new piece, focus on learning it by repeating a phrase at a time, keeping it in tempo as much as possible. Practicing something out of time to get it in time is usually an inefficient use of your efforts, and a signal that you need to isolate specific skills in your practice routine.

Exploring Classical Mandolin is designed primarily to help players from different backgrounds explore the rich traditions of classical mandolin. I think you will find the starting points within the book to be both accessible and rewarding, and the advanced parts to be challenging, while illustrating our instrument's potential. Enjoy!

ABOUT THE AUDIO, VIDEO, AND EXTRA NOTATION FILES

This book also includes accompanying audio examples and video demonstrations. To access the accompanying media, go to www.halleonard.com/mylibrary and enter the code found on the first page of this book. This will grant you instant access to every example. Examples with accompanying media are marked with icons. Some examples include additional notation in the online PDF when mandolin ensemble arrangements include other instruments, such as guitar parts.

 Audio

 Video

 Extra Notation Online

PART I

Practice Method for
Contemporary Classical Mandolin

CHAPTER 1

Classical Mandolin Today and Tomorrow

A LIVING TRADITION: WHY NOW IS A GREAT TIME TO BE A MANDOLINIST

Classical mandolin is a contemporary musical language with deep traditions. There is a diverse repertoire of music composed for mandolin, and also a tradition of arranging to mandolin from other instruments. Classical mandolin's improvisational traditions, although rarely heard today, also suggest new paths for exploration.

Classical mandolin's repertoire is strong in modern and Romantic styles, but there is also beautiful mandolin music from the Classical and Baroque eras, and even more music being written today. The dawning of the twentieth century brought both popularity and virtuoso approaches to mandolin, and left us a repertoire awaiting rediscovery. Both eighteenth and nineteenth century methods contributed techniques—many are now virtually forgotten or only in the hands of classical mandolin specialists—that shed new light on future possibilities.

For a worldwide community of mandolinists, newly connected to each other and to their instrumental traditions, the creative possibilities are endless. Here is a quick listing of the currents of mandolin music that have contributed to this book.

- *Current practice.* Italy, Germany, Japan, and the United States—and perhaps others—have each produced distinct ways of playing and thinking about the mandolin. This book will introduce some of those ideas, with practical exercises to help you get them into your playing.

- *Earlier methods.* Through the years, interesting ideas about how to play the mandolin have fallen in and out of fashion and are underrepresented in current practice. This book will illuminate some interesting and forward-looking avenues to explore, based in our rich traditions—plus some new, original music using these techniques.

- *The Virtuoso Era.* Mandolin virtuosos, in the second half of the nineteenth century, brought a level of technique to their performances in Italy and across Europe and America that is rarely remembered today. The skill level declined again as this knowledge was lost early in the twentieth century, but some of the great virtuosos (particularly Calace, Munier, and Ranieri) left behind method books that remain indispensible to anyone interested in the technical potential of the mandolin.

- *The Golden Era.* Late in the Virtuoso Era, a wave of mandolin popularity in America merged the sounds of ragtime, jazz, and Tin Pan Alley with classical mandolin. This nearly forgotten repertoire, and the techniques invented to play it, offers fresh perspectives and is essential to any improvising mandolinist who wishes to understand the roots of the American mandolin.

- *Baroque Music.* Vivaldi's mandolin concerti are often remembered, but they are just part of a vast repertoire of Baroque mandolin music. Baroque mandolin concerti range from moderately easy to virtuosic, and recent recoveries have brought to light previously forgotten Baroque works. (Have a look at Barbella's "Allegro" for two mandolins on page 78.)

- *Folk Traditions.* More than perhaps any other instrument, classical mandolin is deeply entwined with folk music traditions. Some folk traditions such as Neapolitan and Lombardian folk song have had a symbiotic relationship with classical mandolin, and mandolin styles within some others (Ticino music, choro, Sicilian) show a strong classical influence. Adapting popular songs is an old tradition amongst classical mandolinists, and pleasing the audience with familiar melodies is not the only reason: folk sources can provide rich vocabularies for new composition.

- *The Classical Era.* Several surviving books document delightful and idiomatic ways of playing the mandolin. These eighteenth century tutors offer new paths of exploration today, among them books by Gervasio, Denis, Leone, Corrette, and Fouchetti. My own techniques have been deeply influenced by these authors, and combining their ideas with jazz and contemporary classical vocabulary forms the basis of my compositions in this book.

Understanding the deep traditions of our instrument offers a valuable perspective on the potential of our instrument!

INTERNATIONAL SCHOOLS OF THOUGHT

Today, it's easy to hear the differences between mandolinists who have studied through the various national traditions of classical mandolin, among them German, Italian, French, Japanese, and American. In his book *The Classical Mandolin,*[1] Paul Sparks described these differing schools of thought and traced their development. In the intervening decades between the publishing of *The Classical Mandolin* and this one, several important developments have occurred.

In recent decades, Germany has seen a meteoric rise of the mandolin within its educational system. German visionaries have not only redesigned the Italian mandolin in service of their own national musical aesthetic; they have created

[1] Sparks, Paul, *The Classical Mandolin.* Oxford University Press, 1995, 2005.

a robust infrastructure for educating and developing young players within this approach.

Mandolin, meanwhile, has thrived in the Far East. Mandolin orchestras have achieved a high artistic level in Japan, Korea, and Taiwan. Japanese luthiers are making top-level instruments, and two composer/performer/teachers—Jiri Nakano and Yasuo Kuwahara—have composed new works and methodologies building on the achievements of the nineteenth century virtuosos while extending their own very personal compositional vocabularies. Maestro Nakano also built a vast collection of international mandolin repertoire that has helped to spread mandolin pedagogy and ensemble music around the world.

In Holland, the revival of a deep tradition—the Roman school of the Italian classical mandolin—has exposed new potential, and even given us a glimpse of the nearly forgotten achievements of previous generations. Based on the research, teaching, and mentorship of Alex Timmerman, the orchestra Het Consort has produced young virtuosos and developed an exquisitely subtle timbral blend. The implications for tonal possibilities of the mandolin-guitar orchestra—and thus the potential range of musical expression within this idiom—can be fully appreciated only in live performance of this ensemble.

Another interesting development has occurred recently in Israel. A single mentor, Lev Khaimovich, has cultivated a group of young mandolinists, some of whom are now mature artists. Their instrument, the Kerman mandolin, is a modern update of a flat, double-topped design. Avi Avital is the best known of the young Israeli mandolinists, and he is the first mandolinist to record for the prestigious label Deutsche Grammophon.

In the United States, a trend toward America's earlier mandolin traditions—classical, blues, and string-band music—is visible. Meanwhile, another mandolinist—Chris Thile—has captured the imagination of mandolin fans, and brought a new level of mainstream visibility to our instrument while simultaneously pushing its boundaries. His 2011 award of the MacArthur "genius" grant has brought new attention to the mandolin from different levels of society, and helped to bring about renewed awareness of mandolin in the public consciousness. Thile's interpretations of the Bach solo sonatas and partitas for violin have connected the Gibson F5 mandolin—best known as the icon of bluegrass mandolin—to its original intent, the interpretation of classical (and popular) repertoire.

MANDOLIN'S "BIG BANG": THE FIGARO SPANISH STUDENTS

The Spanish Students was a touring ensemble that enjoyed a brief but influential popularity around 1880. They dressed in colorful traditional Spanish costumes and performed folk songs and popular classical melodies with great skill and showmanship. They played guitars, bandurria, and other traditional instruments of Spain, but their lasting contribution came from the imitators they inspired. Among those were the "Figaro Spanish Students"—the first of many Italian ensembles drawing on a great wealth of virtuoso Italian mandolin music—who spread the popularity of the mandolin and its classical traditions across both Europe and America. By the time the "Spanish Students" fad passed, America's first generation of professional mandolinist/teachers had become well-established, aided by the great popularity of mandolin in amateur music-making.[2]

CHOOSING YOUR INSTRUMENT

Classical music is played on a range of very different instruments. To highlight the possibilities:

1. *Neapolitan mandolin.* This (along with the Roman design) is the popular bowlback mandolin, for which most eighteenth and nineteenth century repertoire was composed. Various refinements have been introduced through the centuries, but the design featuring steel strings and the slightly bent (canted) top has been essentially the same since mid-eighteenth century. Recent refinements have produced a new level of warmth and projection.

2. *Roman mandolin.* Closely related to the Neapolitan mandolin, this bowlback instrument also has a long yet distinct tradition, and its designers have introduced improvements such as the v-shaped neck and radiused fingerboard. Roman mandolins also typically have a more trapezoidal-shaped fingerboard with a narrower nut, taller bridge, and more sharply canted soundboard.

3. *The German mandolin.* In the 1980s (borrowing elements of earlier German designs), Reinhold Seiffert and others created a bowlback mandolin with a more rounded shape and a broad, flat fingerboard requiring more guitar-like technique. This instrument normally uses flatwound strings, and is played with a rubber or soft plastic plectrum. The design is a large departure from the Italian mandolin, and favors note fundamentals rather than overtones.

4. *The carved top/back mandolin.* Pioneered in the 1890s by Orville Gibson, this was a radical redesign of the classical mandolin and an attempt to apply European violin design to mandolin and guitar. Carved-top and -back mandolins have been favored by most American classical players (early Lyon and Healy models are especially prized), although today

---

[2] Sparks, pp. 26–27.

the carved design, particularly the iconic Gibson F5, is most associated with bluegrass. Europeans often consider this a "folk mandolin," but the carved-top instrument has earned its place in classical music in the United States.

5. *The flat-top, flat-back mandolin.* Sometimes with canted top, guitar-style bent back, or details borrowed from other designs, this style has sometimes been favored by builders in Germany and central Europe. It is also a popular design for the lower members of the mandolin family: mandola,[3] octave mandolin, and mandocello.

6. *The mandolino and Neapolitan mandolin.* These instruments were once well known in Europe, and predate all of the above designs. Since they were tuned differently than the modern mandolin, adapting their repertoire to the modern EADG tuning can pose technical challenges. Today they are rarely heard, and are used mainly by early music specialists seeking historical authenticity for specific repertory.

7. *Other historical designs.* Several cities of Italy lent their names to precursors of the modern mandolin: Genoa, Naples, Milan, Cremona, and Brescia. These instruments had various tunings and numbers of strings in single- and double-courses, but like the mandolino and Neapolitan mandolin, they are rarely heard today.

LOOKING FORWARD: TAPPING OUR ROOTS

Here is another part of why today is such a great time to play mandolin: there is perhaps no other instrument with such strong, yet nearly forgotten, foundations upon which to build a contemporary perspective. The Virtuoso Era ended before recording technology was able to accurately record the mandolin. Fashions changed, the world was torn apart twice by world war—and somehow, the collective knowledge of mandolin's achievements was lost or forgotten in the face of catastrophic historical events. The history of music, after all, is the history of what happened to be recorded in one form or another.

In the 1940s, the American mandolin found new popularity through the musical vision of Bill Monroe, who not only created a highly popular musical form based in America's folk roots (later known as "bluegrass"), but influenced the development of rock and roll.[4] Mandolin became closely associated with bluegrass, and Orville Gibson's original vision—to build a better classical mandolin—was supplanted in the popular eye by the icon of mandolin in bluegrass.

---

[3] There is little standardization about what is meant by "mandola." In the United States, this usually refers to a lower instrument in CGDA tuning (a design contributed by the Roman luthier Giovanni Battista Maldura in the 1890s), and most American ensemble music is scored for CGDA mandola (also called "mandola in C," "tenor mandola," or "mandoliola"). The European orchestra repertoire, however, is scored mainly for GDAE mandola ("mandola in G," "octave mandola," or "octave mandolin").

[4] Bill Monroe was inducted into the Rock & Roll Hall of Fame in recognition of his broader contributions to American music.

Today, Bill Monroe's contributions remain influential, and ideas developed through successive generations of bluegrass musicians are giving shape to a new form of improvisational chamber music. Classical mandolin is no longer exclusively in the hands of specialists, and the next generation of improvising mandolinists has begun to borrow ideas from classical mandolin. As musical boundaries continue to erode, familiarity with mandolin's rich classical traditions is likely to become even more useful.

When we envision a future that embraces all of our musical and technical traditions, we have the best chance of developing a truly contemporary perspective. Doing so enables us to connect to the earliest roots of the American mandolin, as well as to the international mandolin community where classical mandolin is the predominant dialect.

CHAPTER 2

Classical Techniques

RIGHT-HAND MECHANISMS FOR TONE, SPEED, AND EFFICIENCY

Choosing the Pick

Mandolin strings carry high tension, so you need a fairly heavy pick. There should also be a bit of flexibility to bend with the string. A pick that is too heavy to flex will not help your tremolo, since pick and string flex together,[1] and a too-thin pick won't generate enough energy to produce a full sound. There are, of course, different schools of thought, but the classical world is mostly unified on the preference for a pointed pick (either slightly flexible, or rigid and carefully beveled). Rounded-off points may seem warmer at first, but they do so by removing brilliance (which is not the same as boosting bass response). If you choose equipment designed to produce the full spectrum of sound with a wide range of overtones, you will begin with the widest possible range of tone—and thus expression—available. Any mechanical device that removes brilliance is like putting a mute on your mandolin. Sometimes, it can be a good choice for the moment, but in the long run, you're likely to develop a wider range of expression by learning to control that brilliance with your technique—an endless process of learning to shape the sound.

The debate about overtones is one area where the differences in national schools of thought are most evident. The view I've expressed above about the importance of learning to shape overtones through technique is grounded in the Italian mandolin aesthetic, and it is predominant in the United States and Far East as well. There have, however, been major departures from this way of thinking. The German system that has arisen since the 1980s has produced a warm-sounding mandolin designed to minimize overtones—an idea supported by the use of flatwound strings and rubber (or soft plastic) plectra. American

---

[1] The Roman system offers an alternate view, where the pick is inflexible and large enough to pivot between the thumb and forefinger.

bluegrass mandolinists often use mechanical devices (string grommets, dark-sounding picks) for the same purpose. Whichever sound you prefer, be aware that both the Italian and German systems have highly developed methodologies, and emanate from very different musical aesthetics. This diversity of approaches is to everyone's benefit: mandolin orchestras based in both German and Italian systems can each produce a lush and beautiful sound, but in very different ways.

Pick Noise

To some extent, the noise of pick on string is unavoidable, but classical mandolinists work hard to reduce pick noise. Some picks are inherently noisy, especially those made of dark-sounding material (although beveling sharp edges can help). These picks are sometimes preferred for their warm tone (i.e., lack of brilliance), but a dark-sounding pick also falls into the category of "mandolin mute." There is obviously nothing wrong with putting a mute on your mandolin if you like the results, but this should be a conscious choice.[2] To produce the fullest tonal range, a pick should be bright-sounding so it makes a sharp "ping" when dropped. A pick that lands with a "thud" is probably not delivering a full spectrum of sound.

Holding the Pick

The "pencil grip" is popular among classical mandolinists. Figure 2.1 illustrates the idea: the pick is nearly parallel to the index finger, and nearly perpendicular to the thumb. The pick rests against the soft pad of both the index finger and thumb.

FIG. 2.1. Pencil Grip

---

[2] My own preference is to use a bright pick primarily, sometimes substituting darker picks for specific situations.

I prefer an alternative way of holding the pick used by many American mandolinists, which is sometimes called the "modern pick grip," and can be found in American method books dating back nearly a hundred years.[3] In this method, the pick contacts the side of the index finger, resting on the hard surface of the smaller knuckle. This position may make it easier to maximize your loudness, but it may not facilitate tremolo playing as easily. Of course, these results also depend on your pick choice and hand position.

FIG. 2.2. Modern Pick Grip

A third way of holding the pick is associated with the Roman virtuosos such as Silvio Ranieri. The Roman method relies on a large, inflexible pick that is heavy enough to pivot between the thumb and forefinger. Although virtually forgotten through most of the twentieth century, a new generation of virtuosos such as Ralf Leenen, Sebastiaan de Grebber and Ferdinand Binnendijk have demonstrated new potential in this approach.

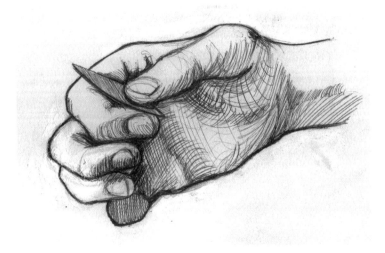

FIG. 2.3. Roman Grip

[3] Bickford, Zarh Myron, *The Bickford Mandolin Method, Vol. 1*. Carl Fischer, New York, 1920.

Whichever way you hold the pick, remember to grip it loosely. When you need to play louder, tighten the grip a bit, without tightening any other part of your right-hand mechanism. Both dynamics and tone are deeply dependent on the way you hold the pick.

PICK/STRING ANGLE

Place your pick so that its flat surface is flat against the string. This is my preferred pick position, but sometimes, I rotate the pick a few degrees clockwise. In this position the pick cuts slightly diagonally across the strings, reducing pick flex. The rotated position can give a little more warmth, but it is also less precise and prone to pick noise. With practice, you may find that the desirable results of the rotated position can also be achieved with pick flat against the string.

Right-Hand Position

Let's consider a second kind of angle: the angle between the flat surface of the pick and the top of your mandolin. Figure 2.4 illustrates what I'll call the "direct" hand position: the right wrist is centered over the strings with the pick pointed directly at the top of the instrument. This position is my starting point, and is very common among modern mandolinists.[4] In this vertical position, the pick can easily reach any string using primarily the wrist mechanism. Easy alternation of upstrokes and downstrokes is possible without changing hand position, and the tonal difference between upstroke and downstroke is minimized.

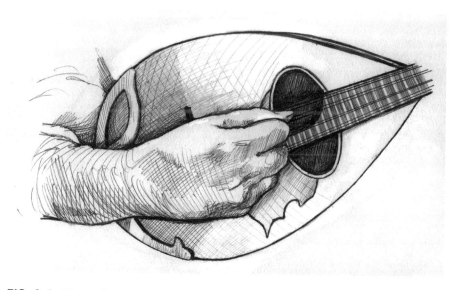

FIG. 2.4. Direct Position

_____

[4] Historical representations of this hand position may be found in methods by Munier, Bickford, and Cottin.

Alternatively, you might point the pick more toward the ceiling by rotating your forearm clockwise, away from you. Figure 2.5 illustrates what I will call "low" hand position, with the hand mostly below the strings and the pick reaching back up, pointed somewhat toward the ceiling. This position achieves a warm tone on the downstroke, and involves some level of forearm rotation. With the hand in "direct" position, i.e. over the strings with the pick pointed directly toward the top of the instrument, pick motion depends more on the wrist and less on rotation of the forearm.

FIG. 2.5. Low Position

Many historical methods illustrate low-hand position.[5] Although the directly-over-the-strings hand position is more common today, some mandolinists alternate the two approaches, contrasting techniques dependent on each.[6] I prefer direct position for free strokes and *string crossings* (silently crossing over a string to approach from the other direction), but I also rely on low position for rest strokes, special effects, and some tremolo.

Planting and Right-Hand Points of Contact

Many mandolin players outside the classical world use the technique of planting the wrist just behind the bridge. To maximize the tonal possibilities, however, I recommend developing a right-hand technique that allows movement freely up and down the string so that your pick can make contact with the strings back by the bridge, up over the fingerboard, or anywhere in between. Some players use contact between the last three fingers of the right hand and the mandolin's top or finger rest to gauge the pick's position relative to the strings. I sometimes brush the back of the curled fingers against the top of the instrument as an additional point of reference, particularly when tremoloing on the E course.

---

[5] Among them, methods by Cristofaro, Koehler, Pietrapertosa, and Vorpahl.
[6] Some of my compositions in this book, such as "Tillamook Impressions," rely on both right-hand positions.

Moving the Pick

To move the pick across the strings, think of using primarily the weight of your hand. To break down the process, pick motion is the result of several mechanisms including the elbow, rotation of forearm (key turning motion), wrist (both hammering and waving motions), and finger movement. Each of these mechanisms has a place in both modern practice and our technical traditions, so we must consider each separately.

- *Elbow.* This is the strongest joint, but also the slowest. It may be used to support the motion of the forearm and wrist, but I don't recommend the elbow as a primary source of motion.

- *Forearm.* Twisting the forearm easily produces rapid pick motion, but in an arc which requires compensation to keep the pick near the strings. Most modern approaches to technique deemphasize this mechanism, but it remains an important part of both practice and tradition, and is indispensible for some musical styles (such as gypsy jazz).[7] I think of both elbow and forearm as slightly moving platforms used to amplify the motion of the wrist.

- *Wrist.* "Wrist motion" can be a source of misunderstanding, since it is sometimes confused with the combined motion of wrist and forearm. The wrist can move in two dimensions, as described above, and (in most modern approaches) is usually flat against the strings or nearby. My approach begins with a flat wrist, close to strings, sometimes aided by just a little forearm rotation. When the pick needs to travel farther (such as when reaching across all four courses), the wrist arches a little more, accompanied with a bit more forearm motion. The rotating wrist/forearm rotation mechanism also comes more into play as the hand moves into low position.

- *Fingers.* Wiggling the pick between thumb and index finger produces poor results for all but the smallest motions, since these joints are small and relatively weak. Hold the pick loosely, firming your grip for louder passages, and don't let the thumb and fingers move. Speed will come as the mechanism becomes more confident. If you can play quickly without finger movement, the thumb and first finger may be used to rotate the pick. This may be done to maintain a consistent angle on the strings as you move across the courses, or to change the tone by making the pick cut diagonally through the strings, edge first.

- *Finding your own way.* There is little standardization in the size and shape of mandolin necks, and scale lengths vary considerably. For this reason, we each have to find our own way, diagnosing problems as we go along—preferably while considering the broader traditions of our instrument, as well as the techniques most popular today!

---

[7] For more on technique, including the arched wrist and twisting forearm, please see the Bickford and Pettine methods.

CLASSIC(AL) MANDOLIN METHODS

Throughout this book, I refer to classic mandolin methods, several of which are available in the public domain. The era of mandolin's greatest popularity—roughly 1880 to 1920—was also the era of great virtuosos, some of whom documented their approaches in method books. Those books were in turn based (at least in part) on developing the knowledge base represented in the eighteenth-century methods. Today, all of these resources can help to unlock the potential of our instrument. They also serve as an entry way to specific learning traditions and their specialized knowledge.

LEARNING TRADITIONS

Everyone has a different opinion, so all you can trust is your own intuition, right? This message often underlies Internet-based learning, but a better way to study any complicated topic is to immerse yourself in a learning tradition, such as a systematic and time-tested method book, or private studies with an experienced teacher. You will be confronted with seemingly contradictory ideas, and balancing one against the other will require questioning your frame of reference—the assumptions underlying our belief systems. Our frame of reference helps us to sort out good ideas from bad, but it also becomes a lens that colors the way we see things. Sometimes, taking a step back from the things we "know" offers a chance to see things in a new light. A broad understanding of the technical traditions of our instrument can only help to illuminate the possibilities!

SOME GENERAL ADVICE

For efficient pick motion, use big joints and muscles for the large movements, and use smaller ones for smaller movements. Most of the work will be done by wrist and/or wrist and forearm together. Be sure that you're not using little joints and muscles to make big movements. Practicing with a mirror can be helpful to understand your own technique and self-diagnose problems.

Don't hesitate to use any of the mechanisms discussed here in developing your technique; remember that our technical traditions are broader than today's most popular techniques. Listen to your intuition, but be willing to question your own beliefs. Remain open to different approaches, and don't expect to always understand the value of each idea in advance. Some will reveal themselves to you only after careful study.

Zen Moment

Put the above mechanisms aside. Once you consider the mechanisms that move the pick, it is even more important not to approach picking as the sum of the movements you're controlling. Instead, focus on the weight of your arm. Try to capture its inertia to move the pick. Think of a tree blowing in the wind—the leaves may move quickly, but that quick motion is the cumulative result of smaller motions distributed through the tree. The trunk moves hardly at all, the large branches, barely perceptibly. You get the idea—the pick can be moved at breathtaking speed, without a lot of work, when the parts are well coordinated.

HONORABLE MENTION: THE ARCHED WRIST

"There is no doubt that the perfectly flat wrist leaves the chords (tendons) the most flexible and allows the broadest wrist motion, but the position most generally adopted is to slightly arch the wrist, from one half to an inch and one half above the bridge." [8]

—H.F. Odell, 1906

To earlier generations the arched wrist position, combined with forearm rotation, was common. Both ideas were used by many early twentieth century mandolin and guitar virtuosos, and can be seen in surviving videos by Dave Apollon and Roy Smeck as well as contemporary masters such as Marilynn Mair and Richard Walz. In recent decades, a trend away from forearm motion has been accompanied by a flattening of the wrist, sometimes compensated by moving the wrist diagonally, simultaneously in both dimensions.

---

[8] Odell, Herbert Forrest, *Odell Method for the Mandolin*. Boston: Oliver Ditson Co., 1906: p. 15.

LEFT-HAND POSITIONING FOR ECONOMY

Figure 2.6 illustrates left-hand position: the fingers are curved so that fingertips contact the fingerboard, and are held diagonally at approximately a 45-degree angle to the neck. The left thumb points up toward the headstock, also at a 45-degree angle, and is usually held opposite of the second finger.[9] Notice also that the thumb is contacting the side (not the back) of the v-shaped neck. The v-neck fits into the v-shape formed by thumb and index finger. The wrist is held straight, leaving space between the palm of the hand and the back of the neck.

FIG. 2.6. Left-Hand Position

Your left hand will normally move through a range of positions, so please note the changes to left-hand position carefully when you watch the online videos. The guidelines mentioned here are only a starting place, so if, for example, you sometimes find your wrist bending to accommodate a difficult stretch, that exception to the rule might be necessary. If so, keep in mind the longer-term goal of keeping the wrist straight, and perhaps later you will find a better way to make that difficult stretch without bending the wrist. Much depends on the way you hold the mandolin; sometimes raising the entire instrument can facilitate left-hand technique.

Finger Position: Two Approaches

Most American mandolinists (including me!) keep the fingers of the left hand positioned closely over the fingerboard when not in use, to minimize the distance each finger must travel when needed. This approach is well documented in older

---

[9] The German system is based on a different hand position in which the thumb is usually placed behind the neck, and fingers are more parallel to frets.

methods that represent our technical traditions and have shaped the way we think about technique.[10] That economy, however, comes at a price: holding the unused fingers in position close to the fingerboard retains unnecessary tension in the left hand. Some classical mandolinists prefer a less-curved, more relaxed position for the fingers when not in use.

If (like me) you've spent years learning how to keep the fingers always close to the fingerboard, try this: curve the fingers carefully into position close to the fingerboard. Now, freeze your fingers in that position, and lift the hand away from the fingerboard. Feel that tension? Now release the tension, allowing your fingers to partially straighten. The neutral position of the fingers, using neither flexor nor extensor, is not straight but is less curved than before. Now, take that relaxed, less-curved finger position back to the fingerboard, and note how your fingers look: they're partially extended. Some mandolinists prefer this more relaxed position for inactive fingers. Whichever you choose, leaving the fingers down as long as possible will reduce unnecessary motion.

When fretting the string, move the finger by bending the knuckle joint only. The two smaller finger joints should move little, if at all. Exert just enough pressure to hold string to fret. Especially if your instrument has tall, arched frets, it's usually not necessary to push your finger all the way to the wood. (Some builders believe that low, flat frets can be depressed and released faster, but I find that frets that are tall and well crowned facilitate subtleties of articulation.) Pressing too hard on the strings can cause poor intonation, buzzing, and unnecessary fatigue.

These details are the sort that make generalizations difficult, because mandolin necks and setups vary tremendously. Our hand sizes and finger lengths vary even more! Therefore, this description should be taken only as a set of guidelines. I will, however, mention one common source of left-hand problems: some mandolin necks have a rounded shape instead of the more common v-shape. At the lower price points, this is a concession to guitar players who might pick up the mandolin now and then; at the high end, it represents a system of design choices with implications for both right- and left-hand technique. In either case, a rounded mandolin neck (often combined with a wide, flat fingerboard in German and South American instruments) may require that the neck be held higher to get the left hand into an efficient position, as well as a more guitar-like left-hand technique with thumb behind the neck and fingers more parallel to frets.

NOTATING PICK DIRECTION

Throughout this book, pick direction is normally indicated only when changing. When you see pick direction indicated, you can assume that it's a change from what came before.

---

[10] See the Bickford and Odell methods.

SHAPING TONE WITH LEFT AND RIGHT HANDS

Your choice of right-hand position (direct vs. low position, as described previously) impacts your tone. Low position enables a warm and loud downstroke, but positioning the pick vertically over the strings can help to minimize the inherent difference between the sound of downstroke and upstroke. Chapter 3 presents some picking alternatives to broaden your range of tone color. Other right-hand technical factors that influence tone production include pick grip, material, weight, shape, and angle (degree of rotation in relation to both the string and the top of your instrument).

Left-hand factors affecting tone include finger placement relative to fret, and left-hand pressure. These details take a great deal of time and effort to explore. Together, the coordination of the two hands has a great impact on your tone. Strive to relax the hands, using only the tension necessary. Learning to relax unneeded muscles is a long-term goal that will greatly benefit your tone. Right/left-hand coordination is also crucial to creating a smooth, legato sound. Legato playing is one of the most difficult yet important technical challenges on mandolin, requiring us to eliminate the silences between the notes.

Keep in mind that every instrument has a range of tone, but some ranges are wider than others. A good instrument will take time to explore, just to survey the possibilities! We often make the mistake of comparing the tone of one instrument to another, without considering how many variables can affect tone. Whichever way you go, most of the tone is in your hands, so don't get too caught up in thinking you must have this instrument or that one to find the tone you like.

GOING DEEPER

The advice offered here is a summary of current practice, historical perspective, and my own views based on my own years of studying and teaching the technical traditions of mandolin. Every school of thought in the classical mandolin world has specific approaches to technique and tone production, and these ideas are sometimes in conflict with each other (even within the same tradition!). Nothing can help your classical technique more than working closely with a teacher who studied one of these systems. I think of this kind of learning as a folk tradition, with the best surviving ideas of previous generations being passed on by those who have had time to thoroughly digest them. Each new generation of students tries out those ideas, discards some, adds their own, and synthesizes a personal approach.

CHAPTER 3

Picking Patterns and Tremolo

ALTERNATE PICKING

Our exploration of picking patterns begins with alternate picking, a technique often used in classical mandolin,[1] and just as in other musical worlds, mastery is important before moving on to the alternatives. Alternate picking is a pattern in which the pick moves down on the beat, and up off of the beat. Figure 3.1 is an exercise designed to help build your muscle memory for alternate picking.

FIG. 3.1. Alternate Picking Exercise 1

Consistency of pick direction is important: down, down-up, down, down-up. This way, your pick is always moving down on the beat, and up off the beat.

⊓ = *downstroke*

∨ = *upstroke*

FIG. 3.2. Pick Direction Notation

---

[1] To focus on alternate picking within the classical mandolin tradition, you might explore the Cristofaro *Method for Mandolin*, or *The Complete Mandolinist* by Marilynn Mair.

Be careful to keep that pick direction pattern the same as you explore the following variations:

FIG. 3.3. Alternate Picking Exercise 2

Once alternate picking feels natural in figure 3.3, figure 3.4's "Alternate Picking Exercise 3" will continue to develop your alternate picking accuracy over three adjacent courses.

FIG. 3.4. Alternate Picking Exercise 3

When you are comfortable playing figure 3.4, try these variations.

FIG. 3.5. Alternate Picking Exercise 3 (Variations)

As your muscle memory increases, the down, down-up pattern becomes second nature. When you're ready for alternate picking exercises that require more right/left-hand coordination, "Alternate Picking Exercise 4" can incorporate the previous right-hand patterns into your scale practice. Here are some ideas to get you started:

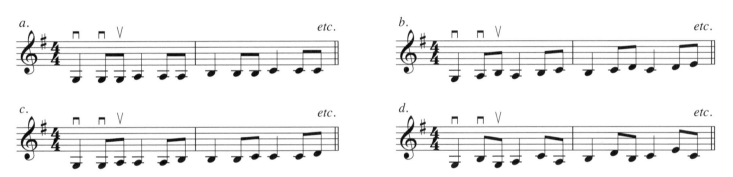

FIG. 3.6. Alternate Picking Exercise 4

Invent your own variations on these patterns. Practice them in all keys, beginning with G, C, D, A, and E major. Transpose to minor keys as well, and also to modes of the major scale. If you're bored with scales, make them more challenging by adding speed bursts, changing rhythms, keys, etc. Scale study should be challenging, rewarding—and fun!

The great advantage of alternate picking is that it speeds learning, since there is no need to memorize new picking patterns for each phrase. Some also prefer this approach because the player can focus on developing right-hand speed, rather than learning new picking patterns for each new piece. When alternate-picking technique is solid, you have a simple right-hand device that can be readily applied to just about any new piece you're learning.

ALTERNATE PICKING WITH SYNCOPATIONS

The following syncopation study will further develop your sense of alternate picking. You may choose to play it with a bit of swing, or use even eighths. Be careful to follow the picking pattern exactly, and apply the pattern by ear to other keys during your scale practice.

Be sure to keep the pick moving during the rests—for example in the first measure, third beat of figure 3.7, the pick should keep moving with a silent down-stroke. The pick doesn't contact the strings on beat 3, but it must keep the down-up motion going so that the next eighth note can be played with an upstroke. Don't go on to other picking patterns until the pick direction, using syncopations, seems intuitive.

FIG. 3.7. Two Syncopation Studies

USING OPEN STRINGS

When reading classical mandolin notation, you normally can assume that notes available on open strings are played open, unless (1) a fingering is otherwise indicated; (2) you are playing higher than first position (see page 45); or (3) the note in question repeats a previously-indicated pattern.

In the first measure of figure 3.7, a fingering indicates that the D is to be played with the fourth finger, instead of the open D string. The reason is tonal consistency: since D is the highest note of this phrase, it would likely stand out if played on the open string. In the following measure, the same note is played on the open string. It's less likely to sound exposed, since here, it occurs within an ascending melodic line.

Figure 3.8, "Alternate Syncopations," adheres strictly to alternate picking: downstrokes fall on beats 1, 2, and 3, and any note between is an upstroke.

FIG. 3.8. Alternate Syncopations

LEFT-HAND FINGERING CONVENTIONS

The music in this book adheres to the standard one-finger-per-scale-degree-rule: When you play a diatonic major or minor scale, each finger plays one note of the scale. Normally, the first finger covers frets 1 and 2; the second, 3 and 4; the third, 5 and 6. The fourth finger is used for notes on fret 7.

These fingerings are only a starting point and apply only in first position (see chapter 4). You can normally assume that notes without written-in fingerings follow this convention, and that notes that do not follow it will have written-in fingerings. The exceptions occur when an unconventional fingering is otherwise clear (such as when it's part of a pre-established pattern), or when written-in fingerings denote a position shift.

FREE STROKES AND REST STROKES

You've probably performed the exercises up to this point with *free stroke* technique; i.e., the pick moves freely and makes contact only when sounding the string. An alternative is the *rest stroke*. The rest stroke emphasizes a single note and can maximize the loudness of your instrument.

Prepare the rest stroke by placing your pick on the string. Push the pick through the string pair, and let it come to rest on the next higher course. Some use this approach for most downstrokes; I prefer to reserve it for special emphasis. Optionally, you may rotate the hand into low position (figure 2.5) to make the rest stroke easier. (In chapter 6, we'll look at a special effect, the half-rest stroke, that relies on this position.) With the right hand in low position, the pick travels more toward the face of the instrument (rather than down toward the floor) making it easier to come to rest on the next course.

Sometimes, the rest stroke is not prepared but begins as a free stroke, ending when the pick comes to rest on the next higher course. Both are useful, but when possible, I usually prefer the prepared rest stroke.

Another possibility is the *prepared free stroke*, which begins the same as a prepared rest stroke but does not come to rest afterward on another course. This is useful when you wish to create a slight emphasis by separating a note from what came before—without the accent of the rest stroke. Whether free stroke or rest stroke, any stroke that starts with your pick on the string creates a slight separation from the previous stroke.

Video
2

Either rest strokes or free strokes may be prepared. Rest strokes are usually prepared; free strokes usually are not. All four possibilities are valuable interpretive tools. In the following video example, listen for how the first note of each four-note group is performed: first with free strokes, then with prepared free strokes, and third with rest strokes. Notice that the left-hand fingering is not identical: a rest stroke is usually followed by an upstroke on the same course (or another rest stroke).

ALTERNATE PICKING ALTERNATIVES

Some schools of thought use alternate picking exclusively, or nearly exclusively. The following alternatives are therefore completely optional, but if you choose to explore them, I think you'll find they expand the tonal palette of the mandolin.

If the pick is pointed directly toward the face of your mandolin (as in figure 2.4), the tonal difference between an upstroke and a downstroke is minimized. Still, since it is inevitable that there is some difference in tone between upstroke and downstroke, let's look at four alternative approaches.

1. Downstrokes Only

A downstrokes-only approach gives you maximum uniformity of tone between notes, so I often use this device to unify a phrase. I normally begin any Classical-era piece with a downstrokes-only approach. The eighteenth century method of Leone suggested that downstrokes-only should always be used unless speed requires resorting to alternate picking; more than a century later, the same view was expressed in the influential method by Bickford.[2]

2. Glide Strokes

⌐⟋ = glide downstroke

⌐⟋V = glide downstroke followed by upstroke

⌐⟋V⟍ = glide downstroke followed by glide upstroke

V⟍ = glide upstroke

V⟍⌐ = glide upstroke followed by downstroke

V⟍⌐⟋ = glide upstroke followed by glide downstroke

FIG. 3.9. Glide Stroke Key

This device involves picking (usually) adjacent courses in the same direction, either upstroke or down, and often includes the use of rest strokes. A *glide downstroke* includes at least two consecutive downstrokes; a *glide upstroke* includes at least two consecutive upstrokes. To practice glide strokes, let's apply a new rhythm to "Alternate Picking Exercise 3."

FIG. 3.10. Glide Stroke Exercise 1

---

[2] Tyler and Sparks, p. 115; Bickford, p. 44. Tyler and Sparks have detailed various historical approaches to pick direction.

Glide strokes usually occur as you pick two adjacent courses in the same direction, but sometimes your pick will skip a course between. In measure 2, beat 3 of figure 3.11, the G-to-B-flat interval should be played the same as all the previous ascending intervals, with a glide downstroke.

Glide Stroke Etude

August Watters

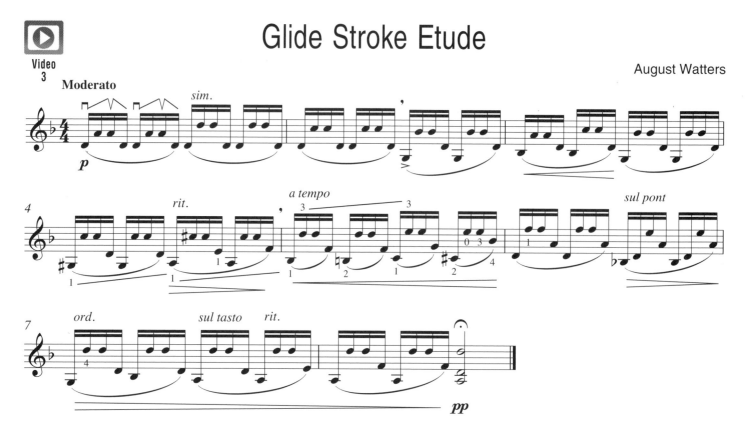

FIG. 3.11. Glide Stroke Etude

Notice the indication "sul pont" in the "Glide Stroke Etude." This indicates that the place where your pick contacts the string should move back toward the bridge, for a brighter sound. "Sul tasto" indicates the opposite; your pick contacts the string over the fingerboard, for a rounder tone. Both indications may be cancelled by "ord."

3. Next-Course Downstrokes

Another useful idiomatic device (documented by Leone in the eighteenth century and by Pettine in 1900)[3] is the idea of using a downstroke every time the pick moves to a different course. This device combines several other devices including alternate picking, glide strokes, and (sometimes) reverse alternate picking. I often use the next-course downstroke approach when I want to strengthen the sound of a line as it ascends or descends.

In figure 3.12, notice how each time the pick travels to a new course, it executes a downstroke. Alternate picking is usually used within each course, but downward glide strokes and other consecutive downstrokes are used when

[3] Leone, *Methode*, pp. 4–5; Pettine, *Pettine's Modern Mandolin School*, Vol. 6, p. 2.]

traveling between courses. As you transpose figure 3.12 to new keys (by ear of course!), your ability to improvise with glide strokes will improve, reducing the learning curve.

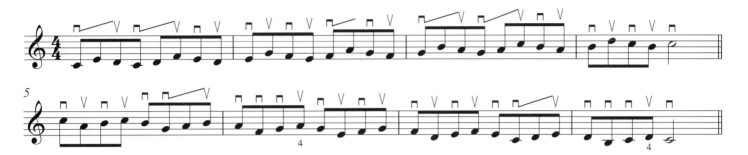

FIG. 3.12. Next-Course Downstrokes

Unless you're completely confident with the scale patterns, don't spend a lot of time at this point memorizing the pick direction. If finding the notes doesn't yet seem intuitive, revert to alternate picking until the locations of the notes you're seeking seem more obvious. Don't try to split your focus between finding the notes and applying glide strokes; one of these needs to be second nature so that you can focus on the other.

"THE FINISHED MANDOLINIST"

Giuseppe Pettine was one of the most influential American mandolinists—an Italian immigrant who lived most of his life in Providence, Rhode Island. The following observation, from his highly-detailed and influential method *Pettine's Modern Mandolin School*, gives us much insight into how we might get the broadest results from our right-hand technique.

Mandolinists. . .might be divided into two classes: . . .those who use a downstroke in changing strings. . . (and) also slide the pick across the strings at every opportunity. . . (and) those that use down and upstrokes alternately, paying no attention whatever to the change of strings. The former hold the pick at an acute angle and generally catch only one string on the upstroke; the latter hold it at a right angle and catch two strings both on the down and upstrokes. **The finished mandolinist must be able to execute in both ways.**[4]

In this quotation, Pettine groups mandolinists into those whose right-hand technique consists of next-course downstrokes and glide strokes, and those who use alternate picking exclusively. His observation about the "acute" pick position of the first group and that they "catch only one string on the upstroke" both imply the use of low hand position. The second group whose members "hold (the pick) at a right angle" implies direct hand position.

Pettine is urging us that, to develop the widest possible range of interpretive skills, we need all of these tools at our disposal: glide strokes, next-course downstrokes, and alternate picking. His descriptions also suggest the importance of both low- and direct hand positions.

---

[4] Pettine, Giuseppe, *Pettine's Modern Mandolin School* Vol. 6, Rhode Island Music Co, Providence RI, 1900, page 2

4. Reverse Alternate Picking

Sometimes, reversing your alternate picking to up-down-up-down will aid the uniformity of sound by reducing string crossings.

Reverse Picking Etude

August Watters

FIG. 3.13. Reverse Picking Etude

"Princess Dorian" uses several approaches to pick direction: alternate picking, reverse alternate picking, glide strokes, and all downstrokes. Memorizing the pick direction along with the notes will help get these devices into your technical vocabulary.

Princess Dorian

August Watters

FIG. 3.14. Princess Dorian

Incorporating alternatives to alternate picking can sometimes help to create a more legato sound appropriate to specific situations. In the following example, I have added some alternative picking ideas to the climactic moments of Bach's "Prelude No. 1 in G Major" for cello (transposed here to D major for mandolin).

Figure 3.15 begins with alternate picking. The pick direction reverses at the end of measure 37 as the melodic line climbs. The glide strokes in measure 39 emulate the slur of the bow (in Bach's original notation, the second, third, and fourth notes of measure 39) playing legato. In this example, mixing several different picking approaches (alternate picking, reverse alternate picking, and glide strokes) helps us to expand the tonal palette of the mandolin.

FIG. 3.15. J.S. Bach "Prelude No. 1 in G Major" Excerpt

MEMORIZING PICK DIRECTION

By now, you've probably noticed a difficulty inherent in mixing different approaches to pick direction: Memorizing the pick direction of every note in a piece is a lot of work, and adds an entirely new dimension of memorization to learning a new piece. This kind of memorization is heavily based in muscle memory, so when you're learning a new piece, be sure to learn just a little bit at a time and come back to it often, phrase by phrase. If you're planning to make this a central part of your playing, you may want to master figures 3.10 and 3.12 so that you can use alternative picking approaches in a more improvisational way, relying less on memorization. You can learn to improvise fingerings and pick direction as you use other approaches, just as you do when you're alternate picking.

TRIPLET PICKING

Just like "jig picking" in Celtic music, single triplets in classical music are usually picked down-up-down. I usually prefer to pick two consecutive triplets down-up-down/up-down-up.

Figure 3.16 demonstrates three ways to pick triplets or other groups of threes: my usual down-up-down/up-down-up (for two consecutive triplets), plus all downstrokes and glide strokes.

Three Ways to Pick Threes

August Watters

FIG. 3.16. Three Ways to Pick Threes

The last chord of figure 3.16 uses a *split-string chord*; the middle notes E and F are played by splitting the D course. For now, it's fine to simplify any split-string chord by omitting the lower of the two split-string notes. In this example, omit the E and play the chord as A F D.

BUILDING FACILITY WITH TREMOLO

Tremolo can be used to create a crescendo or diminuendo, or to vary the timbre of a long note. In either case, the goal is to create the illusion of a sustained sound.

Before we get into the specifics of how to use the tremolo, let's focus on developing right-hand speed. The alternate picking exercises in figures 3.1 to 3.6 use the idea of *speed bursts*: isolated areas of greater activity. Those exercises used only the quarter-eighth-eighth rhythm, and the two eighth notes were our speed burst. Next, we will increase the burst activity to four sixteenth notes. Following are three different rhythmic motives to increase your right-hand speed.

FIG. 3.17. Core Rhythms with Speed Bursts

Figure 3.18 applies three core rhythms to scales, simplifying the left hand so we can focus on the right hand. Set the tempo slow enough that you can play the speed burst accurately (with your metronome, of course!), but fast enough that the burst would not be sustainable unless approached as we have here, mixed with less-active rhythmic figures. Here are some ideas to get you started.

FIG. 3.18. Core Rhythms Applied to Scales

Focus first on applying these rhythmic motives to simple scales, as in figure 3.18, or to just the open strings. To keep it interesting, combine these rhythmic motives to your scale and arpeggio practice. Make up your own variations and explore diatonic and chromatic approach note patterns similar to the ones in figure 3.19. Be sure that the left hand is simplified enough that the exercise remains focused on the right hand, rather than on left/right-hand coordination.

FIG. 3.19. Core Rhythms Applied to More Active Scales with Approach Notes

TREMOLO TECHNIQUE

Perhaps the most common approach to tremolo uses free strokes in both directions, which may be performed with the right hand directly over the strings (figure 2.4). In this case, the pick is perpendicular to the top of the mandolin, minimizing the tonal difference between upstroke and downstroke.

Some mandolinists use a tremolo that sounds two strings on the downstroke and one string on the upstroke. The downstroke may be performed with a rest stroke, which helps the pick to spring back up to contact just the lower string on the upstroke. This two-down, one-up technique is easier to do with the hand in low position. I use tremolo in both hand positions. I also occasionally use a one-down, one-up tremolo (split string trill) as a special effect, usually in conjunction with split-string technique. (See chapter 6.)

TYPES OF TREMOLO

Measured tremolo results when a long note is subdivided into shorter, equal notes repeated to create the appearance of a single sustained note. The tremolo may be any duration from an eighth note to a thirty-second note, or even smaller subdivisions of the beat. Experiment with our core rhythms in figures 3.17, 3.18, and 3.19, using speed bursts in thirty-second notes.

Unmeasured Tremolo. This is a subtly different sound, in which the speed of the tremolo is unrelated to the underlying pulse. The speed of this tremolo may be determined by technical factors, such as the limitations of the right-hand technique, or it may change speed during its duration. A good unmeasured tremolo is usually executed at the fastest comfortable speed, and the player simply ends the tremolo when (or slightly before) the next beat arrives.

Measured tremolo with rubato. This expressive device sounds a lot like unmeasured tremolo: both make the pick attack less noticeable by avoiding even subdivisions of the beat. Although measured tremolo (by definition) is felt in relation to the underlying pulse, it is possible to subtly change the speed of that tremolo without losing the underlying relationship to the pulse. This sense of pushing and pulling against the tempo can create dramatic tension by first establishing the listener's expectations, and then doing something unexpected. This device can also be heard in the bluegrass world; David Grisman is a master!

WHEN TO TREMOLO

Although the use of tremolo is always a matter of personal taste, stylistic conventions of the music often influence our choices. Tremolo is so common in Romantic Italian mandolin music that it is usually assumed to apply to any eighth note or longer, unless a staccato dot is indicated. (Slurs are used to connect one tremoloed note to the next; otherwise, a slight separation is implied.) Classical-era music had its own varieties of tremolo, which are documented in the eighteenth-century methods,[5] in which notes were sometimes extended with tremolo but not connected. The convention in more modern music is for the composer to write in tremolo where required or to leave that choice to the performer.

These are, of course, generalizations, and your ear should always be the guide—once you understand the stylistic conventions of the music. Every musical

[5] Tyler and Sparks, pp. 119–121

work has a context through which it is heard, so communicating with the listeners depends in part on considering what they expect to hear. The unique beauty of earlier musical styles is often best revealed when we appreciate them from their own perspective, rather than through the lens of today's music.

USING THE TREMOLO

My preferred approach to tremolo includes both measured and non-measured varieties, and arose from my attempts to hide the sound of the pick. Rather than clearly defined attacks in measured time, the idea here is to create an illusion, as much as is possible on the mandolin, of a sustained sound.

I often begin a piece using a measured tremolo, and vary the tremolo speed more as the piece develops. I also like to begin a long tremoloed note quietly, and then quickly swell, letting the note blossom behind the beat. Sometimes, I sound a note on the beat, and then quickly begin a tremolo at a low dynamic, gradually increasing in both loudness and speed. The device attempts to mislead the ear to perceive the tremoloed note as a continuation of that first on-the-beat note. This illusion may be supported by the use of sympathetic vibrations from the other strings, or by the way you phrase with other instruments.

There are other times when you'll want to take a more straightforward approach with measured tremolo—for example, when phrasing with other mandolins or playing duo-style (see chapter 6). A straightforward non-measured tremolo is very popular in today's current practice. There is no reason not to cultivate different approaches; each can bring a different flavor.

TREMOLO DYNAMICS

Dynamics in the tremolo are achieved mainly by gripping the pick more or less firmly. To create a crescendo, begin with an extremely loose grip and gradually tighten until you reach your normally loose pick grip.

TREMOLO SPEED

Tremolo need not always be played quickly. Sometimes, the most effective tremolo uses a slower speed! My tremolo normally changes speeds within the duration of each note, and may even change from measured (changing speed but still heard in relation to the pulse) to non-measured.

MOVING TREMOLO BETWEEN COURSES

Crossing to a different course in mid-tremolo can often be avoided via position shifting. When moving to a new course in mid-tremolo is necessary, a smoother effect can be created by approaching each new course with an upstroke, rather than a downstroke. Figure 3.20 contains some ideas for practicing your tremoloed string crossings. As you cross to each new course with an upstroke, take care to play the first note quietly to deemphasize the change in timbre.

The goal here is the opposite of figure 3.12 (where the pick executes a downstroke when traveling to a different course), but the reasoning is the same: the upstroke sounds weaker than the downstroke, especially when changing to a different course. In figure 3.20, the weaker upstroke forms a transition to the next course. As you approach each new course with an upstroke, relax your pick grip a bit just for a moment to soften the transition.

FIG. 3.20. Preparation Exercises for Tremoloed String Crossings

THE TRILL

The trill is a rapid alternation of two pitches. It is important to Baroque music, and easy to overdo in other styles. The Baroque trill normally starts on the diatonic note above the notated pitch, and borrows time from the duration of that note rather than sounding before. The eighteenth-century methods agree that the right hand must pluck each note of the trill,[6] but some modern instruments (particularly with the longer scale of the American design) may yield adequate results with a hammer/pull approach to the trill. Although modern players use the trill freely in Baroque music, many eighteenth-century mandolinists considered this to be an impractical technique for mandolin.[7]

The most difficult part of developing the trill is developing adequate coordination between the hands. To diagnose flaws in your timing, try this exercise.

FIG. 3.21. Preparation Exercise for the Trill

Play figure 3.21 slowly at first to make sure the note G sounds cleanly, with a distinct beginning and end. As you increase the tempo, listen carefully: does the beginning or ending of the note become sloppy? Use your own ears to diagnose the problem. Is your second finger a bit early, or a bit late, to sound the note G?

[6] Tyler and Sparks, p. 122

[7] ibid

COORDINATING THE HANDS
Tonal Considerations

Not enough is said about how hand coordination impacts tone production. Some guidelines:

1. Be sure your left hand is placed lightly but firmly, just behind the fret. The strings need a firm connection to the fret to transfer maximum energy, so take care that your finger doesn't creep backward toward the next-lower fret.

2. Cultivate an awareness of the way the fret feels, rather than pushing all the way down to the wood of the fingerboard.

3. Practice leaving the fingers of the left hand down as long as possible when fretting the note. This affects perceived tone, not just timing, of the note.

4. Relax the picking hand as much as possible. Revisit the picking technique descriptions in chapter 2, and regularly check the setup to make sure your instrument is functioning optimally.

Legato

One of the most difficult skills needed for classical mandolin is the ability to connect the notes, without tremolo. It is a subtle matter of timing to create a smooth melodic line, and there are a number of technical factors that can get in the way.

1. *Moving between courses.* Moving from one course to the next makes it difficult to connect two notes sonically, both because of the different timbres of adjacent strings and the technical challenge of eliminating the space between the notes (especially during the tremolo!).

2. *Position shifts.* Shifting positions without calling attention to the shift is not easy. Of course it is dramatic to slide into a higher position, but you also need to be able to hide the sound of a position shift when desired. To some degree, shifting on the half step (figure 4.17) can eliminate this problem. This technique enables you to take a diagonal approach to the fingerboard, rather than always playing across one position and shifting up only when higher notes are needed.

3. *Pick noise.* Even with all the above technical problems solved, excessive pick noise can interrupt the connecting of notes.

Although our instrument is less legato than a bowed instrument, to a great degree, this can be addressed through the subtleties of technique.

> ### INTERPRETING TREMOLO MARKINGS
> You may notice in the recordings of this book that tremolos sometimes sound more active than their notation indicates. This sometimes happens when picking patterns, like the ones we'll explore in chapter 5, are substituted. Once you internalize those patterns, you'll find great expressive potential in using them the way a harp uses glissandi, to fill out chords.

Figure 3.22 raises the question of how to interpret tremolos when more than one string is sounding, which I will address in chapter 6. Notice that in the streamed video I play the "Tremolo and Trill Etude" the first time through as written, with the tremolo applied only to the highest note. As the recording continues, you can hear ideas for how multi-string tremolos can develop the piece.

Tremolo and Trill Etude

August Watters

Video
7

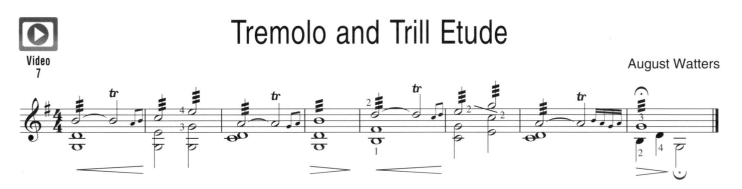

FIG. 3.22. Tremolo and Trill Etude

CHAPTER 4

Intervals and Foundation Exercises

Fluency in performing diatonic intervals throughout the mandolin's range makes reading and memorization much easier. The best way to build this fluency is to focus first on the kinesthetic and aural experience: instead of reading just the notes, focus on visualizing the distances between the notes and associating those visual patterns on the fingerboard with sounds. This chapter presents ideas for building excellent sight-reading skills, mentally "hearing" the notes before you play them, and building technical and conceptual mastery of the fingerboard.

SCALE PATTERNS AND MELODIC INVERSION

Figure 4.1 introduces a simple scale pattern, along with its *inversion*: the same pattern upside-down. Notice that the pattern begins with a diatonic third (C to E). As the four-note pattern climbs, focus on how that diatonic interval (C to E, D to F, E to G, etc.) looks and sounds. Play both patterns, and then transpose by ear to the keys of D major and G major.

FIG. 4.1. Scale Pattern with Inversion

IMPROVISATION AND INTERPRETATION

Throughout this book, you will find ideas about how improvisation can be used as an interpretive tool. The improvisational traditions within classical music can lead us toward more personal approaches to interpreting music, but they also raise questions about when and how often to depart from the written page. My compositions in this book may be interpreted literally as written, or you may find ways to reinterpret them using ideas presented in chapters 3, 4, 5, and 6. I have included a few examples of reinterpretation in the online recordings of these pieces, most often by varying the picking pattern being applied to a chord voicing.

SCALES AND AUDIATION

Although reading scale patterns forms the core of many practice methods, a more direct path toward internalizing scale patterns—and connecting them to your ear—lies in analyzing intervallic patterns relative to the key and applying those patterns by ear to the fingerboard. The goal is to master diatonic intervals first (just the notes in the scale, before you introduce chromatics) by beginning with easy patterns and gradually introducing wider leaps and approach notes. By approaching this process by ear, you're building an ear-to-finger connection fundamental to both sight-reading and improvisation skills.

With that goal in mind, work out the scale patterns in figure 4.2 first as written, and then extending the patterns by ear to cover a wider range (one or two octaves). Transpose to all keys, major and minor. Invent your own patterns in thirds and fourths, and alter them with leaps in fifths and sixths.

FIG. 4.2. Scale Patterns for Practice

Approach scale patterns such as these not just as technical exercises, but also as conceptual exercises to help you envision diatonic intervals as they move through the scale. The patterns in figure 4.2 are a good place to start, but you may need to make them easier or more difficult to keep them challenging yet accessible. As these patterns become engrained in your musical vocabulary, you can use them as a key to new technical challenges.

MULTIPLE STOPS WITH OPEN STRINGS

Sounding notes together on both closed and open strings is an excellent tool for developing your right- and left-hand coordination and building a well-connected legato sound. "Freedom Dance" requires both single and double stops to be sustained, along with an open string. Focus on holding the accompaniment notes full value while also connecting the melody notes. Be careful to observe the phrasing marks, so that the slurred notes are sustained together.

Freedom Dance

August Watters

FIG. 4.3. Freedom Dance

SCALE PATTERNS IN DOUBLE STOPS

Scale patterns in double stops (especially thirds and sixths) introduce technical and conceptual challenges often seen in classical mandolin literature. Since scale patterns using double stops in sixths are easy to play without shifting up the neck, we'll begin with a scale pattern in sixths using open strings.

FIG. 4.4. Scale Patterns Using Double Stops in Sixths

The fingerings in figure 4.4 are not the only correct way to play these notes. They are designed, however, to help you work on your legato playing. As you move from one double stop to the next, one finger must quickly move to an adjacent course. Between the first two pairs of quarter notes, for example, the third finger must quickly move from the G to the C. Play this exercise in strict time, holding the G as long as possible before releasing and moving to the C. As you continue, focus on connecting each double stop to the next in the same way, eliminating the silence between the notes. Work on your right-hand technique too, by getting the double stops to sound as one. Use these double-stop exercises to build your legato sound.

Figure 4.5 adds a picking pattern using the glide stroke. Approach this as you did figure 4.4, taking great care to play smoothly and eliminate the spaces between the notes.

FIG. 4.5. Double-Stop Picking Exercise in Sixths

CLOSED-POSITION SCALES

To play in all keys, you'll need to be equally comfortable with closed-position scales. Mandolin players often play closed-position scales using one of two fingerings as shown in figure 4.6, labeled (a) and (b) above and below the staff:

Video 9

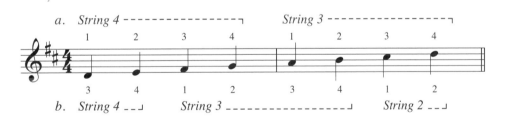

FIG. 4.6. Scale Fingerings Starting on Fingers 1 and 3

Using the string/fingering combination above the staff, the first finger begins the scale on the 7th fret. In the below-the-staff example, the scale begins with the third finger. Both are good ways of playing the scale, but for flexibility we need to be able to begin a scale with any finger, not just the first and third. Before going farther, be sure you can play the scale patterns in figure 4.2, using the D major fingerings of figure 4.6. Transpose by ear to all keys, including minor keys.

Next, here are two more scale fingerings to work into your practice routine, starting respectively with the second and fourth fingers.

Video
9

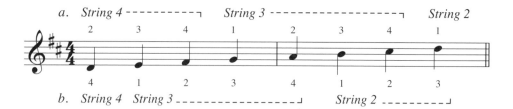

FIG. 4.7. Scale Fingerings Starting on Fingers 2 and 4

If you are not yet familiar with the fingerings in figure 4.7, plug them into your practice routine by extending this D scale across the fingerboard (without shifting up or down), then transposing to new keys using the same fingerings. Next, choose a simple tune you know well by ear and play it using the same approach: root on the D, first finger, and the rest of the notes following by ear without position shifts. Repeat with first note D beginning with fingers 2, 3, and 4. Part III of this book has several simple melodies for this purpose such as "Ode to Joy" and "Simple Gifts." Choose one you know well and play it in all keys, using all four fingering patterns.

When you can play the D scale in all four fingerings, next take the C major patterns from figure 4.2 and transpose them by ear to the key of D, using all four of the fingering patterns in figures 4.6 and 4.7. Once you have mastered all four fingering choices, you can begin a scale on any finger—instead of just the first and third.[1]

CLOSED-POSITION PATTERNS USING DOUBLE STOPS

Figure 4.8 is similar to the scale pattern in sixths from figure 4.5, but it has been moved up the neck so that the first note D sounds on the seventh fret of the G string. Follow the pattern, envisioning the fingering relationships identically as they were in figure 4.5 (where they began on the open D course).

FIG. 4.8. Double-Stop Picking Exercise in Sixths, Closed Position

---

[1] Author Ted Eschliman has written some excellent exercises he calls his "FFcP system." The central idea is that for technical fluency, we need to break the habit of leaping around the fingerboard to find identical fingerings in a different place. Knowing more fingering patterns increases efficiency of motion.

When you can play figure 4.8 as written, apply the fingering patterns from figures 4.6 and 4.7. The objective is to be able to start the exercise on any left-hand finger, and play through the pattern without shifting up or down the neck.

Figure 4.9 introduces double-stop scale patterns in thirds. The fingerings indicated explore a few different possibilities. As before, hold each double stop as long as possible, releasing at the last moment to connect as smoothly as possible to the next.

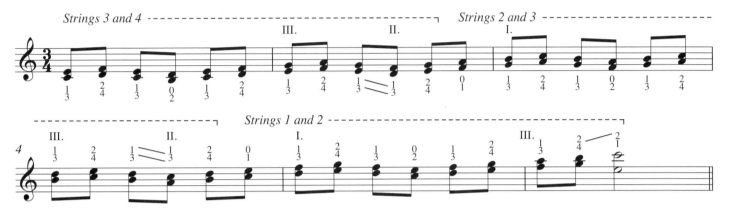

FIG. 4.9. Double-Stop Exercise in Thirds

As with all the previous exercises, practice figure 4.9 first as written, and then transpose it to other keys. Be sure to invent descending patterns too. The real value of these exercises is making them your own! These patterns will be extremely helpful to you in reading classical mandolin music.

Double-Stop Etude

August Watters

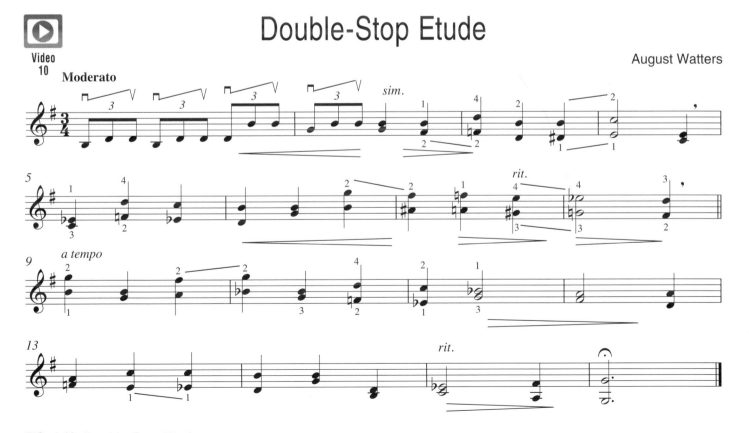

FIG. 4.10. Double-Stop Etude

ARPEGGIO PATTERNS

Although chord arpeggios are sometimes treated as a purely technical exercise, they are also valuable for building an ear-to-finger connections. First, practice to become comfortable with the arpeggio patterns in figure 4.11 (a and b). The fingerings there are based on two different ideas. Follow the fingering indications closely. The Roman numerals indicate positions, so if you haven't yet studied position playing please skip ahead to the next section. When you understand the mechanisms here, transpose both exercises to all keys major and minor, beginning with the key of G.

FIG. 4.11. Arpeggio Fingering Study

Next, memorize the following arpeggio pattern, outlining a D G A D progression. To transpose it to other keys you may need to write it out, but it's worth your time. Figure 4.12 outlines the most common melodic connections between these common chord changes. Internalizing the ear-to-finger connections between these sounds will help you with improvising over any harmonically based music, especially the theme-and-variations variety introduced in chapter 6.

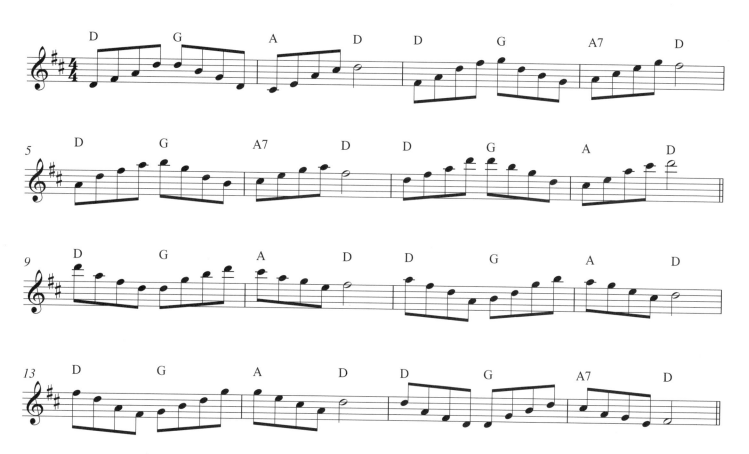

FIG. 4.12. Arpeggio/Voice Leading Study

POSITION PLAYING

Figures 4.6, 4.7, and 4.8 introduced closed-position scale shapes that can be moved up and down the neck. In earlier chapters, the music was easily playable without moving up the neck. Before we go farther, we need an easy system for organizing up-the-neck playing.

In classical mandolin notation, fingerings are usually indicated to shift up or down the neck. If no fingerings are indicated, you can expect to stay in your current position. You need to be fluent with the one-finger-per-diatonic-note guideline mentioned in chapter 3, so if you have any questions about the fingerings in the Paganini composition in figure 4.13, please revisit the scale exercises in chapter 3.

If you haven't thought about the neck in terms of positions, envision the G on your E string, 3rd fret. Normally, you'd play that with your second finger (and we'd call that first position). If you instead play that G with your first finger (where your second finger usually falls), you are now in second position. Thus, the position name (at least for the first four positions) corresponds with the location where your first, second, third, or fourth finger normally rests.

Position Playing: The Thought Process Illustrated

Several classic mandolin methods (and many violin methods!) contain exercises for position shifting,[2] so for our purposes, we'll outline the thought process. Paganini composed a few works for mandolin (Paganini was a great mandolinist too!), and his "Allegro Moderato" is an excellent position-shifting study.

Allegro Moderato

Nicolo Paganini
Edited by August Watters

FIG. 4.13. Position Shifting Study: Paganini's "Allegro Moderato"

---

[2] For example, those by Calace, Branzoli, Krempl, Pietrapertosa, and Schick.

Position Shifting

The opening section of "Allegro Moderato" falls comfortably in first position. Since we normally use one finger per note of the diatonic scale, we'll begin the first two notes, A♯ and B, with fingers 3 and 4. This need not be indicated because it's in first position—you can assume first position is your "default setting" until otherwise indicated. The E in measure 1 is played on the open string since we normally use open strings unless otherwise indicated.

Measure 7 indicates the E is to be played with finger 4 (rather than the open E). Previous E notes were unmarked, and thus assumed to be played on the open string. Two notes later, we reach down to the A♯ and slide back to B. Our first full position shift, though, is in measure 11. There is an indication to play the B with the first finger (where the fourth finger normally rests), so we'll call this fourth position. Think of that B (now under your first finger) as the fifth degree of the key, with your fourth finger now falling on the root (high E). That fifth-to-root relationship—a perfect fourth between fingers 1 and 4—is a very useful way of organizing that part of the scale.

The melody note A at the end of measure 12 is not marked, thus you need to continue in fourth position to play the A with your fourth finger on the second string. Once again, consider the perfect-fourth relationship, this time on the second string with your first finger on the root of the key (E) and the fourth finger on the fourth degree (A). Continue in fourth position until the open E in measure 13, followed by an indication to play the D with your third finger. If the D is to be played with the third finger, the only logical place (barring unnecessary gymnastics) is on the second string—and so, this is an indication to return to first position.

Measure 24 has an indication to play that same D, this time with the second finger (second position). Continue in second position for two measures, until you see the indication to shift from B to C on the third finger. The high note D is now within reach. That last shift (to third position) demonstrates an extremely useful device for shifting positions: the half-step shift. Figure 4.17 will illustrate a new way to practice your scales, shifting on the half step. This way you're going up the neck diagonally, shifting a bit at a time, and minimizing the timbral differences as you go.

Position Shifting with Tremolo

"The Romantic Fourth" illustrates how the tremolo, so often heard in Romantic mandolin music, can affect our left-hand fingering choices. Its first two measures outline a perfect fourth interval (the distance between fingers 1 and 4), first ascending, then descending. The position markers (indicated by Roman numerals) are redundant, but included at this point for extra clarity. If you can play the scale patterns in figure 4.2 in positions I through VI in the key of C, you are ready to study "The Romantic Fourth."

The Romantic Fourth

August Watters

Note fingering relationships
for perfect fourths:

FIG. 4.14. The Romantic Fourth

It's important to notice how the phrasing marks work: they cross barlines and connect what came before to beat 1 of the next measure. Especially in a Romantic (or Neo-Romantic) style, this phrasing structure affects our left-hand fingering choices. When possible, we'll try to keep notes phrased together on the same course, reducing the need to change courses in mid-phrase. As a result, we sometimes need to shift not just to reach higher notes, but also to maintain consistency of tone and remove unnecessary technical obstacles. Of course it's also important to cultivate the skill of changing courses inaudibly!

"The Romantic Fourth" begins with a perfect fourth interval on the E string in second position (scale degree 5 to 1 of the key). Perfect fourth intervals are bracketed throughout, to help you visualize them. The next measure moves that same fingering over one course, where the fourth-to-first finger interval now outlines scale degrees 4 to 1 of the key. The first position shift comes in measure 10, with an indication to reach for the F. We interpret this to mean the F on the first course, since it's closer than the F on the second course, and first position is our "default setting."

The E note in measure 11 might have been played on the open string, without requiring a position shift, but I chose to indicate that note to be played with the first finger to match the warmer tone implied by the dynamic marking. (In classical mandolin music, dynamic markings are often interpreted as instructions for tone as much as loudness.) Reaching for the E note with the first finger places us on the second course, fourth position.

The next phrase (measure 13) indicates that the first finger is to play the C, which we interpret as a move to fifth position.[3] Measure 14 brings a half-step shift on the third finger, to sixth position. Notice that the G note that begins measure 17, when played as indicated with the first finger, could have been played without a position change. Therefore, to indicate that the G should be played on the first course, it is necessary to add *sul Mi*. This is borrowed from fixed-Do solfege, which we often see in the titles of classical compositions. Vivaldi's "Concerto in sol maggiore" is Italian for "Concerto in G Major." Fortunately, there are only four to remember: "sul Mi" means "on the E string," "sul La" means "on the A string," "sul Re" means "on the D string," and "sul Sol" means "on the G string."

WHEN TO SHIFT POSITIONS

The choice of when to shift positions depends to some degree on the style of music you're playing. For Baroque music, I tend to play mainly in first position, shifting up only to reach higher notes on the first two courses. Romantic music requires a more diagonal approach to the fingerboard, in which frequent position shifts help to maintain consistent timbre across the strings by reducing the number of string crossings.[4] Carlo Munier's "Romanzetta" on page 83 offers an excellent example of Romantic-style interpretation using frequent position shifts to maintain consistent timbre.

HALF POSITION

Half position is an alternative that facilitates the execution of notes on the low frets. In half position, the first finger covers the first fret, the second finger frets 2 and 3, the third finger frets 3 and 4, and the fourth finger frets 5 and 6. Figure 4.15 introduces a fingering for the key of B major, using half position in the lower register. When you can apply the scale patterns from figure 4.2 to figure 4.15, you're ready to move on to figure 4.16, John Goodin's *Deer Tracks* "June 2, 2004," which uses quite a bit of half position.

FIG. 4.15. B Major Scale in Half Position

---

[3] If you're comfortable with intervals, another way to think about positions is to calculate the diatonic interval between the open string and your first finger, and subtract 1. In this case, E to C is a sixth, so subtracting one means you're in fifth position.

[4] Flatwound strings minimize the timbral differences between strings, and thus may reduce the need for position shifts. Still, I prefer round-wound strings for their full spectrum of overtones.

June 2, 2004
from *Deer Tracks*

John Goodin
Ed. August Watters

FIG. 4.16. *Deer Tracks*: "June 2, 2004"

BUILDING A DIAGONAL APPROACH TO THE FINGERBOARD

Figure 4.17 presents four exercises to help you move up and across the fingerboard at the same time. It involves building position shifts into the way you move across the neck, shifting up a little at a time with the shape of the melodic line.

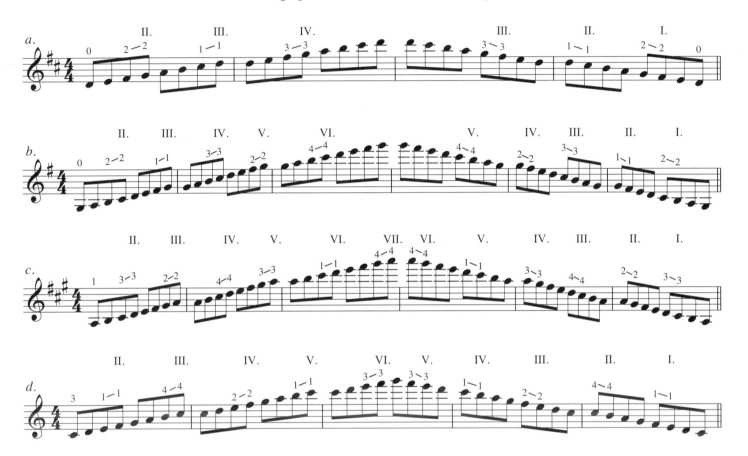

FIG. 4.17. Exercises for Shifting on the Half Step

Once you are able to play the scales in figure 4.17 evenly, apply the intervallic patterns in figure 4.2. Soon, you'll find yourself making decisions on the fly about when to shift and becoming more confident with all areas of the fingerboard.

BUILDING YOUR PRACTICE ROUTINE

These chapters have introduced quite a few exercises, so let's discuss how to best organize them during your practice time. I divide my own practice time into four categories.

1. *Technical and conceptual exercises.* This includes scales, arpeggios, and any other exercise based on musical vocabulary instead of actual repertoire.

2. *New repertoire.* This consists of music I don't yet know, or may be considering adding. Exploring new music is one of the real joys of my practice routine!

3. *Old repertoire.* This includes memorized pieces and reading repertoire (pieces that are active in my repertoire, not committed to memory).

4. *Improvisation.* In classical music, improvisation is usually either the theme-and-variations variety, or it can be melodic ornamentation. Classical mandolin also has a tradition of improvised accompaniments.[5] Chapters 5 and 6 will introduce some ideas for practicing these types of improvisation.

To organize my practice time, I find it helpful to keep a non-digital clock on hand, so that the hands give a graphic representation of how much time I have spent on each task. In the morning, I spend 15 to 20 minutes on each of the four categories, taking care to rest briefly between each. Once the routine is completed, any additional time is spent on the demands of my schedule: preparing concert repertoire, or writing new exercises and etudes to address specific problems. For me, morning practice is best for working on new ideas; night-time is good for maintaining established repertoire.

However you choose to use your practice time, I highly recommend building it into a routine such as the one I have outlined, but adjusted to match your own goals. Keep it fresh and interesting by alternating exercises or repertoire within each category. Organizing your time into regular segments helps you to set short-term goals and measure your progress. A few more thoughts on practicing:

1. Keep a mirror on hand to help you self-diagnose technical problems.

2. If practicing your favorite pieces becomes tiring, try playing in strict time without dynamic changes. It's tiring to invest yourself completely every time you play the music, so take the expressiveness away sometimes and play just for technique. It's less tiring, and the music will be easier next time!

3. Approach technical exercises not just as calisthenics to build technique, but as an opportunity to build your conceptual understanding of your instrument. Keep it fresh, interesting, and fun!

4. Don't repeat too often what you already do well.

5. Segment your practice time, and set short-term goals so that practicing gives you a sense of achievement every day.

6. Practice slowly, and focus on building muscle memory. Loop short phrases to reinforce learning.

7. Come back to the same piece often. Success is more a result of how often you come back to a piece than how much time you spend each time you return.

8. Take short breaks every 15 to 20 minutes, and quit before you are overly tired!

[5] See the picking patterns applied to chords in Leone's method.

READING MUSIC: UPPING YOUR GAME

Classical mandolin requires excellent music reading skills. To break this down into its components, we need to be able to:

1. Recognize the notes, both by name and in context of the key.

2. Be able to read the intervals from one note to the next.

3. Be able to mentally "hear"—or *audiate*—these sounds before ever performing them on an instrument.

Building ability in all three areas is part of developing excellent music reading skills, and it is common to find that one's music education skipped past one or two of these steps! Here are a few recommendations for advancing your reading skills.

1. *Reading intervals.* Don't spend too much energy thinking about the spelling of each note, but focus instead on reading the distances between the notes. Many classical methods begin by moving an interval of a third diatonically through a scale and then gradually expanding to fourths, fifths, sixths, etc.[6] I recommend working through intervallic exercises both by reading and by ear. Before you begin reading through pages of such exercises, however, I recommend mastering the scale patterns in figure 4.2. This helps to lay the foundation for intervallic reading.

2. *Pitch recognition.* Automatically perceiving the scale degree of a note (i.e., its distance from the key center) comes with time. Arpeggio and scale sequence exercises are great ways to expand this skill. Focus on the root of each arpeggio and how the shapes fall in relation to each root. Another good approach is to take a song you know well by ear, and write it out in scale degrees. For example, the melodic phrase "Santa Claus Is Coming to Town" can be written as 3-5-1-3-2-4-7-1.

3. *Audiate.* Mentally "hearing" the pitch, rhythm, and phrasing of written music is a long-term goal. The objective is to see a written note and to associate that visual image with its sound before you play the note on your instrument. The notation, in other words, should not just trigger a technical response that produces the note; it should cause you to hear a note in your ear, which produces the technical response that plays the note. It's a similar process to improvisation: envision, hear, play. If your technique is producing the note mechanically while bypassing the ear, you have it backwards; this is a formula for, well, formulaic playing! Of course the visual aspect of understanding the fingerboard layout is important too and we all rely on this, but to transcend the technical limitations of any instrument it is important to work on hearing what you play, and playing what you hear.

---

[6] Methods in the public domain that begin by working on gradually expanding scale sequences include those by Calace, Branzoli, Odell, Schick, Köhler, and Monti.

CHAPTER 5

Chord Vocabulary and Compound Picking Patterns

To get into the core of classical-style picking, let's now turn to chord vocabulary using longer and more elaborated picking patterns combining alternate picking with other approaches. These patterns will help to explore the timbral potential of our instrument. This chapter will also introduce essential chord vocabulary and a concept for understanding chord-melody relationships. Visualizing the mandolin's neck as an interlocking pattern of triadic shapes can also be very helpful to reading and recognition skills.

Figure 5.1 indicates D-U-D-U alternate picking, using free strokes. The alternate pattern (notated in parentheses) of a glide downstroke followed by an upstroke is likely to be played with three downward rest strokes (or two rest strokes and a downward free stroke), followed by an upstroke. Work through this exercise with both picking patterns, focusing on even tone and connecting the notes as smoothly as possible. There's no question that the two picking approaches sound different!

FIG. 5.1. Picking Exercise with Chord Progression

The inherent difference between the sound of an upstroke and a downstroke is the reason I recommend developing a repertoire of different picking patterns to produce a wider range of sounds. Alternate picking is a good place to begin, but mastering the subtle tonal differences produced by different picking approaches will help you to develop a broader and more expressive tonal palette. Before delving into the possibilities, here's a chord summary of the previous exercise.

Video 12

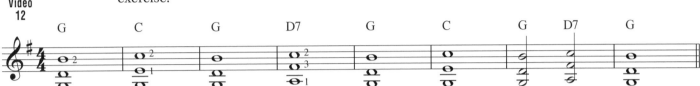

FIG. 5.2. Chord Summary 1 of Figure 5.1

Figure 5.2 is similar to figure 5.1 but has been simplified. Notice how elegantly the fingerings move from one chord to the next. It's not essential that you follow the indicated fingerings exactly, but do give some thought to the guiding finger idea (figure 5.5), to minimize extra motion in the left hand.

Now, let's apply more picking patterns to the same progression.

Video 12

FIG. 5.3. More Picking Patterns for Chord Summary 1, Figure 5.2

Each of the nine patterns above should be applied to the first chord of figure 5.2. Next, keep the same picking pattern going while the left hand moves through the rest of the figure 5.2 chord progression. Don't try to play fast. Make all the notes sound even, and try to eliminate the silences between the notes. While you're focusing on evenness of tone, notice how you're voicing the chord progression: the first chord was voiced G D B, with the B—the third of the chord—voiced in the top. Each subsequent chord is chosen to ensure smooth voice leading (i.e., the last note of each measure moves to the nearest note in the next chord). The chord progression can be analyzed like this:

I   IV

I   V

I   IV

I   V   I

TWO MORE POSSIBILITIES

Video
12

In the figure 5.2 "Chord Summary 1," the first chord was voiced with the third in the lead (so-called because it's usually easiest to hear the highest note). If there are three notes in a triad, it follows that there are two more possibilities: the root or fifth could also have been the lead note. Visualizing all three triad shapes—and being able to voice-lead through a chord progression using them—is the first step toward a fluent chord/melody concept.

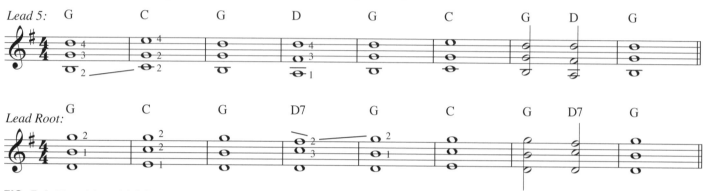

FIG. 5.4. Two More Voicing Possibilities for Figure 5.2

Next, apply all the picking patterns in figure 5.3—previously applied to figure 5.2 "Chord Summary 1"—to the two new voicing possibilities in figure 5.4. Once you can play our simple progression in all three inversions (figures 5.2 and 5.4), transpose them (without writing them out) to new keys, beginning by moving up the neck to A major. Next, move to the major keys of C, D, and F by moving the voicings around the neck—using the top note to organize your thought process ("key of F—lead note 5 of the I chord, find the C, and apply the 'lead 5' triad shape").[1]

CHORD VOCABULARY

Together, figures 5.2 and 5.4 present the core chord vocabulary. As your chord knowledge grows, almost all of your chord voicings can be envisioned in relation to these few chord shapes. Internalizing this chord vocabulary will be immensely helpful in reading music, understanding the fingerboard, and in writing your own arrangements. It will also help with finding fingerings for much of the music in this book.

I have arranged an "Allegro" from Telemann's solo flute minuets, adding mandolinistic chord voicings to illustrate the chord/melody style (page 138), since this approach is so natural to mandolin. Once you're comfortable with those, try working through the mandolin 2 part of Beethoven's "Adagio" (page 102), Calace's "Silvia" (page 107), or Morris's "Dream On" (page 117).

---

[1] If this thought process is not yet understandable, go back to figure 5.2 and label each note of each chord, top to bottom, by function (which part of the chord is it? Root, 3, or 5?). The first four measures are: G (3 5 R), C (R 3 5), G (3 5 R), D7 (7 3 5). Continue the process with figure 5.4. Once you work through this and associate the shape of each chord voicing with its lead note, you won't have to think about it.

GUIDING FINGER PRINCIPLE

The Guiding Finger Principle is an idea to increase your left hand's economy of motion. It applies equally to double stops and chords. The basic idea is that when moving up and down the neck, one finger serves as a pivot point by sliding up and down the string while the other fingers lift as necessary to reach their next desired fret. In other words, all fingers of the left hand should not be lifting off the strings at the same time if possible. When changing chords, the objective is to keep one finger on the same course from one chord to the next, and use it as a pivot point while lifting the other fingers. Finding a pivot point is not always possible, but keeping one finger on the same course to connect two voicings, when possible, can help you to play chords more smoothly.

Any finger can be used as a guide to the next chord. Try to find the common fingers used from one chord to the next on the same course. Occasionally you will encounter a chord change where the guiding finger idea is impossible, when two consecutive chord voicings have no common fingers on the same course. When changing inversions and moving chords up and down the neck, the guiding finger principle will simplify fingerings and facilitate quick chord changes.

Video 13

FIG. 5.5. The Guiding Finger Principle

You'll need multiple fingerings for your chords, depending on what comes before and after. You may play the first chord above (fingerings 3-2) with fingers 2-1 or even 3-1. All are good choices, but I've chosen 3-2 in this case because of the specific voicing that follows. In other words, your exact choice of fingerings for familiar chords may change to facilitate moving to the next chord. Good economy of motion often depends on your ability to find common fingerings when moving between chords.

Without writing them out, apply the Guiding Finger Principle by transposing figure 5.5 up two frets, to the key of D. While you're memorizing the chord shapes, be sure to also associate those shapes with their highest note. (In other words, the first chord is a C triad with the root as highest note, and the second chord is a C triad with the third as the highest note.) Next, transpose by ear to the keys of G, F, and A. The objective is to be able to visualize all three inversions of each triad, on both courses 4-3-2 and 3-2-1. You need all inversions of each chord.

Chord Voicing Etude

August Watters

FIG. 5.6. Chord Voicing Etude

COMPOUND-PICKING PATTERNS IN MANDOLIN MUSIC

A *compound-picking pattern* includes three or more notes. The longest compound pattern in figure 5.3 is eight notes, but some of the picking patterns by eighteenth century composers Denis and Leone are as long as ten or twelve notes! These longer patterns can be found in mandolin music of all eras. The historical method books of Leone, Denis, and Gervasio all contain delightful music based on these patterns. Raffaele Calace brought compound picking ideas into the modern era with his Mount Everest–like *Preludes*, and many modern composers have developed the idea farther including Nakano, Kuwahara, and Wilden-Hüsgen, to name just a few. Most of my own compositions in this book are based on compound-picking patterns, and freely substituting one pattern for another can add an improvisational element to the music.

Before you go farther, take some time to work through Denis's "De la Reine de Golconde," on page 84. This simple melody is elaborated with two variations, demonstrating how compound-picking patterns can be used to lend interest and variety to even the simplest tunes.

"Lullaby for Greta" (figure 5.7) is a tune built on a simple D-D-U pattern, using a more sophisticated harmonic vocabulary. The two downstrokes that begin each pattern do not always fall on adjacent courses, so your pick will sometimes have to jump over a course (for example, the first two notes of the tune!).

Lullaby for Greta

Video
15

August Watters

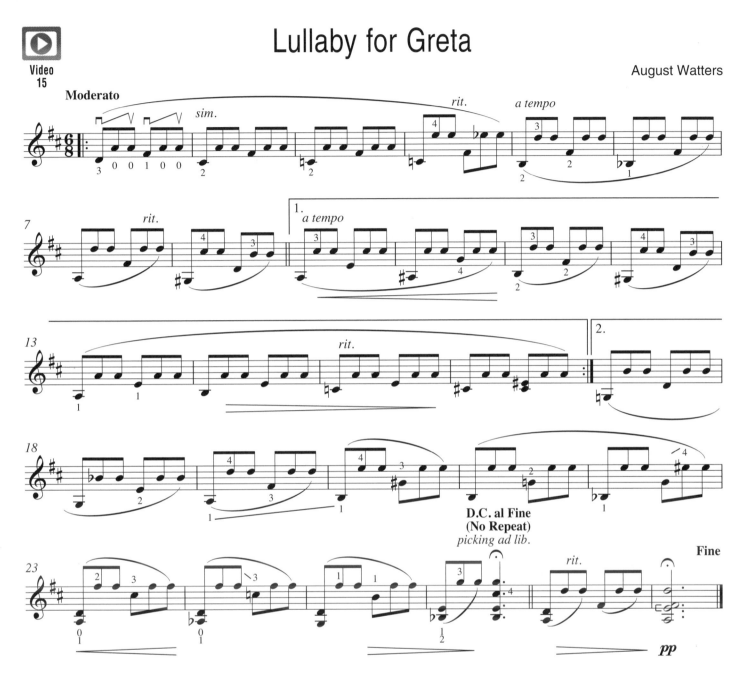

FIG. 5.7. Lullaby for Greta

Notice the indication "picking ad lib." This means that when you reach the D.C. (and return to the beginning), you may substitute any picking pattern. Since this tune does not break the D-D-U picking pattern, you can easily substitute a different picking pattern over the same chord structure. This is one way to approach improvisation! If you've worked through Calace's "Moto Perpetuo" on pages 104–105, take another look at measures 33 through 47. There are also many places in my compositions where improvised picking patterns can bring something new, so there's no need to always interpret the notation literally. Now, revisit figures 3.11, 4.10, and 5.6, and try applying different picking patterns from figure 5.3. You may need to change the written rhythms slightly to make it work, but the exercise will illustrate how interesting variations can be generated just by your choice of picking pattern.

If you wish to pursue the harmonic vocabulary of "Lullaby for Greta," what's needed is a way of playing four-note chord structures, three notes at a time. Jazz players often use this device for accompaniment. Eddie Lang and Freddie Green both used this system in the early days of jazz guitar, and the three-out-of-four note approach works well on mandolin too—Jethro Burns was the master! Ragtime and early jazz were part of the vocabulary of mandolinists during the early days of classical mandolin's popularity in America, so jazz-like chord structures are a natural direction for classical mandolin today.

To introduce three-note voicings of four-note chords, let's revisit our figure 5.2 chord progression. This time, we'll still use triadic structures for the main "on-the-beat" chords, but the second chord in each measure may imply a four-note chord structure (seventh chords) through our choice of notes. In other words, the second chord of each measure is built on a four-note-per-chord structure, even though only three notes are used. One has been omitted to maintain three-note texture throughout.

Video 12

FIG. 5.8. Chord Summary 2: Seventh Chords

As with the previous chord summaries in figures 5.2 and 5.4, you should begin this new chord summary by applying the compound-picking patterns from figure 5.3. Notice that the first chord in figure 5.8 is identical to the first chord in figure 5.2: it's a triad voiced with the third on top. What follows, in figure 5.8, is a voice-led elaboration of our simple progression, this time, with *passing chords* (chords that make a smoother transition to the next chord sound).

I	(I7)	IV	(IVmi)
I	(#Idim)	IImi	V
I	(I7)	IV	(IVmi)
I	V7	IMa7	V7(♭9)

Work through this first elaboration carefully, noticing how each chord leads to the next, and familiarizing yourself with the fingerings. The fingerings indicated are not the only correct fingerings, but they will help to minimize excessive left-hand movement. When you're comfortable, go on to the other two inversions of figure 5.8 (lead 5 and lead root). Notice that the passing chords are slightly different from one inversion to the next (i.e., the second chord of the "lead 5" inversion is G augmented instead of G7). Once you work through all of these inversions and begin to transpose to new keys, your ear will begin to substitute one for the other. Now you have both tools!

It's important to know your triads first: if you're working through the figure 5.8 voicings, make sure that you are envisioning them as variations on the basic triad sounds of figure 5.2. Now that you have some experience with the various picking patterns in figure 5.3, you should begin to improvise through the progressions using different picking patterns.

The chord vocabulary materials in this chapter are most closely associated with the language of ragtime and jazz, which were part of the early twentieth-century American classical mandolin repertoire. Parts II and III also contain examples of works by Beethoven (page 100) and Calace (page 104) that use the same chord vocabulary. I'm confident this approach also belongs to the future of classical mandolin!

The Golden Era

August Watters

FIG. 5.9. The Golden Era

CHAPTER 6

Advanced Concepts

IMPROVISING IN THE CLASSICAL STYLE

You've probably heard these anecdotes: Mozart and Beethoven were great improvisers. Bach was the first jazz musician. Paganini was a great showman who dazzled audiences with improvised cadenzas. These stories hint at some of the improvisational languages within the western classical tradition, and also at future possibilities for improvising classical musicians.

A theme-and-variations approach to improvisation was well known to earlier generations of classical musicians. A similar approach to composition is well represented in mandolin literature, but the ways in which the technique may have entered common practice in the form of improvisation is largely a matter of conjecture. Still, it is reasonable to suppose that mastery of theme-and-variations improvisation could have contributed to the glowing accounts of early twentieth-century American virtuosos such as Samuel Siegel, Aubrey Stauffer, and Seth Weeks.

Today, it is possible to reconstruct an improvisational approach to classical mandolin by deconstructing the theme-and-variations technique within our own repertory. Whether improvised or composed, the devices used to create melodic variations can be seen in an eighteenth-century mandolin composition by Pietro Denis, "De la Reine de Golconde" (the complete composition, with variations, can be found on page 84).

De la Reine de Golconde
Structural Analysis

Pietro Denis

FIG. 6.1. Structural Analysis of "De la Reine de Golconde"

In figure 6.1, the first few measures of "De la Reine de Golconde" has been reduced to a skeletal melody. Schenkerian analysis calls these the "background" notes, but old-time fiddlers know them as "corners"—the elemental notes that form the melody's basic structure. The "corner" melody is still recognizable since it outlines the melodic shape, and the variations are built upon that simplified melody.

Variation 1 begins by quoting the first four notes of the melody directly, and then decorating the simplified melodic line with arpeggios of the implied chords. "Corner" notes quoted within the variation always sound somewhere within their original duration, although sometimes they are slightly delayed. There is one note in Variation 1 for each note of the original melody, so we can say there is a 1:1 textural relationship.

Variation 2 is built on running sixteenth notes, so there is a 2:1 (or more exactly, 6:3) relationship to the original melody. Like Variation 1, most of the melodic motion consists of arpeggio notes borrowed from the implied harmony, but this four-measure phrase also adds melodic ornamentation in the form of repeated notes and a trill-like figure resolving to the melody note E at the phrase's end.

Improvising variations is a matter of "hearing" the structural melody in your inner ear while also knitting together those structural notes with embellishments such as the ones we identified in the Denis composition. This type of improvising variations lives on in folk traditions, such as Texas-style fiddling. This style is of course different than classical improvisation, but the techniques used to generate variations (melodic ornamentation, arpeggios, rhythmic texture) are very much the same.

Improvising requires excellent ear-to-finger connections, so that as your inner ear "hears" the improvised notes you are about to play, your technique automatically produces them on the fingerboard. Musicians whose training has focused on interpreting written notes via the instrumental techniques used to produce them are at a disadvantage, since the ear connection in that process is secondary. For most students of improvisation, that critical ear-to-finger relationship must be built through practice materials such as the scale sequence and arpeggio exercises in earlier chapters of this book.

Figure 6.2 outlines an improvisation exercise based on my tune "Three Ways to Pick Threes" (figure 3.16). In the video of improvised variations on this melody, I explore two ways of improvising using 4:3 and 2:1 rhythmic textures to help generate melodic ideas. Listen for the way those rhythmic textures suggest embellishments, including arpeggios and melodic ornamentation.

FIG. 6.2. Improvisation Exercise on "Three Ways to Pick Threes"

Figure 6.3 presents a few scale exercise ideas to help you develop a sense for using approach notes. I have matched the key, time signature, and tempo to Paganini's "Allegro Moderato," to help you match your variations to this piece.

If you have internalized the scale and arpeggio exercises in previous chapters of this book, these approach-note patterns should be within reach.

FIG. 6.3. Approach Note Exercises for Paganini

DUO-STYLE

Duo-style playing was popularized by American players such as Bickford, Stauffer, and Pettine in the early 1900s, and also can be found in the work of the Italian masters Calace and Munier. It's an approach that makes one mandolin sound like two, usually by tremoloing a melody note (with a measured tremolo) while picking single accompaniment notes beneath. The Golden Era duo-style music features the sounds of ragtime and early jazz as well as classical sounds built on the eighteenth- and nineteenth-century masters, but twentieth- and twenty-first-century composers have updated the duo-style approach with a newer harmonic vocabulary. Duo-style mandolin, especially when combined with modern harmonic language, is a whole new way to think about mandolin playing.

To get started with duo-style playing, please return to "Freedom Dance" (figure 4.3). This piece does not use tremolo, but is clearly a duo-style piece divided into melody and accompaniment parts. Next, look at the first measure of "Just the Two of Us," (figure 6.4) where the melody note B in the first beat is tremoloed for three beats. On beats 1, 2 and 3, the pick also reaches down for the lower notes while maintaining an even tremolo on the melody note. The goal here is to create the illusion of a sustained melody note accompanied by a second part, thus "duo-style."

Just the Two of Us

August Watters

FIG. 6.4. Just the Two of Us

The tremolo indications in measures 4 and 5 need not be interpreted literally. I have recorded them with a variety of approaches, some borrowing from the compound-picking patterns in figure 5.3. As your facility with those patterns increases, you may find yourself using them as a harp-like glissando across multiple strings, wherever more than one note is being tremoloed. Compare the written version of "Just the Two of Us" with the recording, for ideas about finding the common ground between tremolo and compound-picking patterns. There's also a recording in chapter 3, "Tremolo and Trill Etude," illustrating how those patterns can be used to fill out chords.

Other examples of duo-style repertoire in this book include pages 106, 112, and 145. For further study, the methods of Carlo Munier and Aubrey Stauffer cover this ground thoroughly, as does Evan Marshall's "Duo-Style A to Z."

SPLITTING THE STRINGS

Split-string technique: the idea of dividing a single course so that each string of a pair is sounding on a different fret. It's rarely done, but it's not as difficult as you think! We know that mandolinists have used this technique for a long time, since it's documented in the eighteenth-century method of Leone.[1] For some classical-era split-string mandolin writing, have a look at the fourth variation of Leone's "La chasse de L'isle adan" on page 94.

Split-string technique is easier with careful preparation of the fingernails. Your nail needs to be just the right length: long enough to make contact with the fingerboard without changing the angle of your finger, but short enough that the main pressure of your finger is still exerted by the finger pad, not the nail. You may want to use an acrylic nail hardener, similar to the way classical guitarists treat their right-hand nails. Applying that hardener to the left-hand

[1] See Leone, page 17

nails creates a firmer surface to grab the string, and toughens the nail enough to stand up against your steel strings. We'll use a fingernail to stop the lower of the two strings in a pair (i.e., the one closer to the floor).

SPLIT-STRING TECHNIQUES PART 1

1. Double stop using open string and first finger (single-string stop)

2. Triple stop using open string plus 3-string stop

FIG. 6.5. Split-String Techniques 1 and 2

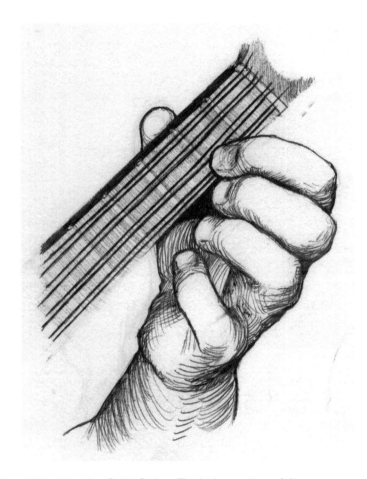

FIG. 6.6. Hand Position for Split-String Techniques 1 and 2

Figure 6.6 illustrates the hand position for both techniques 1 and 2. Notice that the index finger is splitting the A course, with the fingernail depressing just one string (the A string closer to the floor). The other A string vibrates open; thus both the notes A and B are sounded together on the A course. Once you have both the A and B sounding, slide your first finger up to C, D, and E, increasing the size of the interval between the stopped note and the open string.

Technique 2 uses exactly the same left-hand mechanism as in technique 1. Notice that in figure 6.6, the index finger is holding down not only the single A string on the second fret, but also both strings on the first course. If you successfully split the A course in technique 1, your first finger was probably also pressing down on the E strings creating a perfect fifth interval. We'll call this the "three-string stop."

"Split String Etude No. 1" uses techniques 1 and 2 in its first measure: the open A with the B fretted on the second fret, and the F-sharp sounding a perfect fifth above in a three-string stop.

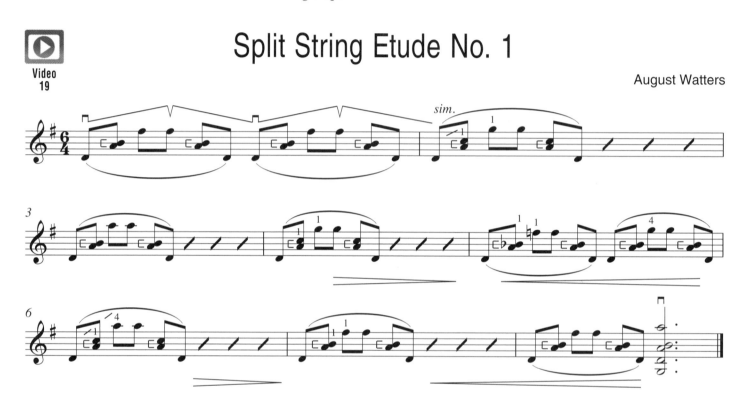

Video 19

Split String Etude No. 1

August Watters

FIG. 6.7. Split String Etude No. 1

SPLIT-STRING TECHNIQUES PART 2

You may have noticed another new technique in "Split String Etude No. 1." In measure 3, the first finger splits the A course on the second fret, but instead of a three-string stop (B F♯) on the first finger, the high A is sounded. Continuing with our list of split-string techniques, we'll call this split-string technique 3.

3. Single-string stop plus higher note, different finger

4. Double stop, closed position, optional higher note

FIG. 6.8. Split-String Techniques No. 3 and No. 4

Split-string technique 3 is similar to 2, as noted, except that the top two strings of a three-string stop do not sound—because a higher note on that same course has been fingered.

Split-string technique 4 is a closed-position version of technique 3; your first finger goes on the lowest note of the course to be split, and your second or third finger frets the note a second or third higher. Optionally, you can also engage your fourth finger to add more choices.

Here's an etude to illustrate techniques 1, 2, and 3.

Split String Etude No. 2

August Watters

* = hold the double stop, and play single notes B-A-B by picking single strings

FIG. 6.9. Split String Etude No. 2

"Split String Etude No. 3" begins with technique 4—a closed-position double stop (E–G on the third course), which in the second measure becomes a three-string stop (F–G) plus a D sounding above.

Split String Etude No. 3

August Watters

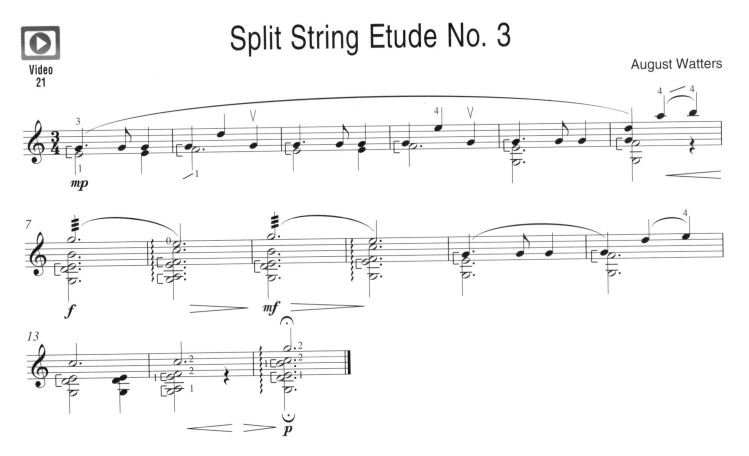

FIG. 6.10. Split String Etude No. 3

SPLIT-STRING TECHNIQUES PART 3

There are two more split-string techniques introduced in the above "Split String Etude No. 3." The last two measures (14 and 15) each use two three-string stops. This is technique 5. Also, measure 10 introduces the idea that open strings (in this case E) can ring on a higher course above a three-string stop. We'll call this technique 6.

5. Two three-string stops

6. Three-string stop plus open strings

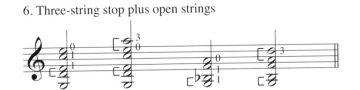

FIG. 6.11. Split-String Techniques 5 and 6

FIG. 6.12. Split-String Technique 5

Figure 6.12 demonstrates the fingering position for the first chord in figure 6.11. This chord uses two three-string stops, and is spelled D-E-B-C-G, from the bottom up. Notice that using two three-string stops results in two internal perfect fifth intervals: E-B and C-G. Technique 6 uses a single three-string stop with additional open strings, and optionally a split course on a higher string. Without a doubt, you'll find more possibilities if you get into exploring these!

Here's a simple exercise for applying the idea of splitting two courses at once. Think of how your left-hand fingers 1 and 2 stay in exact relation to each other as they play the familiar G to C progression in figure 6.13 (a).

Video
22

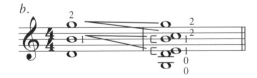

FIG. 6.13. Technique for Splitting Two Courses

Next, keep your fingers in exactly the same relation as when they were changing from the G to the C chord, but instead of moving over one complete course (two strings), move over only one string. Figure 6.13 (b) shows the result: a chord with two split courses.

"Glass on the Beach" is a minimalist composition that will give you a chance to practice your double-split-string chords. The indication "Fine ad lib" is an invitation to improvise the ending as you wish.

Glass on the Beach

August Watters

FIG. 6.14. Glass on the Beach

BUILDING SPLIT-STRING CHORDS

The chords in "Split String Etude No. 3" are built by combining one or two three-string stops with open strings and/or a stopped note. Split-string technique 5 (figure 6.11) is for chords using two three-string stops, sometimes with additional notes. Without too much trouble, you can get five or six notes per chord, but even one split course creates a dramatic change in the mandolin's texture. My most-used split-string texture is a four-note chord on the bottom three courses, with only the D course split. To explore this idea, go back to figures 5.2, 5.4, and 5.8 to experiment with how splitting the middle course of your three-course chord structure can expand your chord vocabulary.

Figure 6.15 presents more chord possibilities to spark your imagination, combining more than one split course. Begin with a single open string, as noted, and layer one note at a time for full, sonorous chords.

FIG. 6.15. Building Split-String Chords

THE HALF-REST STROKE

The half-rest stroke is a picking device much like a rest stroke, but applied to just one string (rather than one course). The technique can be very useful in conjunction with split-string technique. It's not too difficult to do, if you rotate your right hand into low position, and your pick is narrow enough. With your hand in low position, the pick can split any course and come to rest on the lower string of any pair (the one closest to the floor). Measure 3 of "Tillamook Impressions" (figure 6.16) uses this device: the G course is split between the note G, which sounds on beat 1, and the note A sounding on beat 2. There should be no pick movement between the two; your pick performs a rest stroke on only one G string, and sounds the second on beat 2.

THE SPLIT-STRING TRILL

The split-string trill enables the rapid alternation of two different pitches on a single split course. It's based on a right-hand technique that's usually best avoided: the arched wrist directly over the bridge. The arched wrist technique normally requires a certain amount of forearm rotation, but as mentioned in chapter 2, that forearm rotation tends to arc the pick away from the strings. That arc can cause the pick to contact only one string on the downstroke and the other string on the upstroke. Under normal circumstances, this can be a cause of weak tone, but as a special effect, contacting only one string in each direction means we can split the course and alternate two different notes. "Tillamook Impressions" (figure 6.16) uses the split-string trill in measures 29–31 and again in measure 32. "Split String Etude No. 2" (figure 6.9) also uses this device in measure 21.

Tillamook Impressions

August Watters

FIG. 6.16. Tillamook Impressions

USING THE ETUDES IN YOUR PRACTICE ROUTINE

The etudes in this book are designed to address a range of instrumental techniques. One way to get the most from them is to arrange them in an order (such as the one below) designed to help you work toward your musical goals, and then play them daily to maintain and develop your technique.

These etudes will prepare your technique for a wide variety of classical mandolin literature. To advance your technical development, you'll probably still need to dedicate plenty of time to exercises, but playing through your memorized set of etudes every day can help to make technical practice more musical, rewarding, and fun.

PICKING ETUDES	1	"Alternate Syncopations"	p. 23	Alternate picking
	2	"Reverse Picking Etude"	p. 28	Reverse alternate picking
	3	"Glide Stroke Etude"	p. 26	Glide strokes
	4	"Three Ways to Pick Threes"	p. 31	Downstrokes, alternate picking, glide strokes
	5	"Double-Stop Etude"	p. 43	Rest strokes, double stops
	6	"Princess Dorian"	p. 29	Picking summary: alternate, reverse, down, glide strokes
CHORD VOCABULARY	7	"Tremolo and Trill Etude"	p. 37	Interpreting tremolo and trill notation, chord voicings
	8	"Chord Voicing Etude"	p. 58	Chord voicings, glide strokes
	9	"Lullaby for Greta"	p. 59	Chord voicings, compound picking patterns
DUO STYLE	10	"Freedom Dance"	p. 40	Right/left hand coordination
	11	"Just the Two of Us"	p. 66	Duo-style, chord voice leading
	12	"The Golden Era"	p. 61	Duo-style, chord voice leading
SPLIT-STRING ETUDES	13	"Split String Etude No. 1"	p. 68	Split-string techniques 1 and 2
	14	"Split String Etude No. 2"	p. 69	Split-string techniques 3 and 4
	15	"Split String Etude No. 3"	p. 70	Split-string techniques 5 and 6
	16	"Glass on the Beach"	p. 72	Double split-string technique
	17	"Tillamook Impressions"	p. 74	Summary

PART II
Literature of the Classical Mandolin

Part II presents an overview of music composed for classical mandolin including new compositions, works illustrating techniques presented in part I, pieces (some well known, others rarely heard) representing significant musical eras, and important historical works. It is not intended as a representative sampling of classical mandolin literature, but it does include many avenues of exploration into the various subgenres of classical mandolin.

I have minimized the addition of fingerings, dynamics, and other interpretive or technical instruction so that you can find your own interpretation. Part II begins with four relatively easy ensemble pieces, with play-along accompaniment tracks. The following pieces are for solo mandolin, and together present a foundation for further study. Part II ends with several of my own concert works, illustrating how to use some of the more advanced concepts presented in part I, chapters 5 and 6. I hope that part II will bring you many pleasurable hours of music-making, and demonstrate some of the potential of our versatile instrument.

BARBELLA, "ALLEGRO"

Barbella's *Sonata for Two Mandolins and Continuo in G Major* is part of the Gimo collection, named for a small town in Sweden where nineteen works for mandolin, collected in Italy in 1762 but forgotten for two hundred years, were recovered. Their level of difficulty ranges from easy to virtuosic, and their rediscovery hints at the possibility of future recoveries of Baroque-era mandolin repertoire.

Audio
3, 4, 5

Allegro
from *Sonata for Two Mandolins and Continuo in G Major*, Gimo 18

Emanuele Barbella
c. Mid-Eighteenth Century
Ed. August Watters

VIVALDI, "ANDANTE"

This "Andante" is the slow second movement of one of the best known Baroque mandolin concerti, Vivaldi's *Concerto for Two Mandolins* RV532. It was composed for an earlier form of mandolin, probably with gut strings played with the fingers and tuned in fourths, although it also works well in the modern tuning in fifths. This piece emerged from the musical culture of the wealthy Venetian Republic, which in the mid-eighteenth century, controlled Venice, Padua, Verona, and the surrounding Veneto region, as well as Brescia—areas whose rich plucked-instrument traditions included early forms of the mandolin.

Audio
6, 7, 8

Andante
from *Concerto for Two Mandolins*

Antonio Vivaldi
RV532
Ed. August Watters

FOUCHETTI, "MENUETTE"

Giovanni Fouchetti was an eighteenth-century teacher and composer who contributed mandolin music in an elegant, restrained classical style. You may find a few surprising dissonances! Notice the ossia measures above bars 5 and 6. These demonstrate one way an eighteenth-century trill might have been performed, beginning with the diatonic note above the note being trilled. You may choose to add more repetitions of second and third notes (F and G in ossia bar 5) within the same trill, especially when the note being trilled is longer than the quarter note in this example.

Audio
9, 10, 11

Menuette

from *Méthode pour apprendre facilement á jouer de la mandoline á 4 et á 6 cordes*

Giovanni Fouchetti
c. Late Eighteenth Century
Ed. August Watters

MUNIER, "ROMANZETTA"

One of the greatest performers of the Virtuoso Era, Carlo Munier also composed more than three hundred works for mandolin and mandolin ensemble. Munier's "Romanzetta" is an excellent example of Romantic-era mandolin-and-guitar music: there is a wide range of textures and moods to be discovered, although relatively few notes on the page!

Romanzetta

Carlo Munier
Op. 53
Ed. August Watters

DENIS, "DE LA REINE DE GOLCONDE"

Pietro Denis' work documents ornate and delightful ways of playing mandolin in eighteenth-century France, where our instrument was popular among court musicians and the nobility they served. The compound-picking patterns in the first and second variations are excellent devices for exploring the timbral potential of mandolin.

De la Reine de Golconde
from *Méthode pour apprendre à jouer de la mandoline sans mâitre*

Pietro Denis
Ed. August Watters

First Variation

Second Variation

KIOULAPHIDES, "PRELUDE" TO *SUITE FOR ALI*

Victor Kioulaphides' beautiful *Suite for Ali* was composed for Alison Stephens, a brilliant
mandolinist and teacher who left us much too soon.

"Prelude" to *Suite for Ali*

Victor Kioulaphides, 2009
Ed. August Watters

DENIS, SELECTED PRELUDES

The "Preludes" of Pietro Denis are eighteenth-century gems that demonstrate the use of compound-picking patterns (see chapter 5) such as the simple D-D-U glide-stroke pattern of "Prelude No. 1." "Prelude No. 2" also uses a D-D-U glide-stroke pattern, but here the two downstrokes often require skipping over a course (for example, measure 3 begins with a low B♭ moving to a high B♭ in a single pick stroke, requiring us to skip over courses 2 and 3). "Prelude No. 4" is based on a six-note pattern: D-D-D-U-D-U, where the first three notes are played by a single glide stroke. "Preludes No. 6" and "7" introduce patterns as long as twelve notes.

Selected Preludes
from *Méthode pour apprendre à jouer de la mandoline sans maître*

Pietro Denis
c. Late Eighteenth Century
Ed. August Watters

Prelude No. 1

* *This is an abbreviation meaning "apply previous rhythmic pattern to these chords."*

Prelude No. 2

Prelude No. 4

*Slashes mean repeat
the previous two beats
(in this case, six notes).*

Prelude No. 6

Prelude No. 7

LEONE, "LA CHASSE DE L'ISLE ADAN"

Leone's *La Chasse de L'isle adan* is an excellent example of Classical-era theme and variations. The two groups of three eighth notes per measure are usually played D-U-D-U-D-U, although some adjustment may be made to reduce string crossings. Otherwise, the work suggests mainly alternate picking, plus a few compound-picking patterns. Of special interest is variation 4, which suggests split-string technique. Variation 5 contains some ambiguities; I have left them as written for you to interpret.

La Chasse de L'isle adan
from *Méthode raisonnée pour passer du violon à la mandoline
et de l'archet a la plume*

Gabriele Leone
c. Late Eighteenth Century
Ed. August Watters

Leone, "La Chasse de L'isle adan" from *Méthode raisonnée pour passer du violon à la mandoline et de l'archet a la plume*

93

MOYER, "QUEEN OF BEAUTY"

"Queen of Beauty" is a 1920 composition in duo-style by one of the masters of the Golden Era, William Moyer. Notice how the melody is sometimes in the lower voice, and sometimes in the higher. "Queen of Beauty" uses *scordatura* (retuning, in this case, of one string of the second course), so every note on the A course sounds as a double stop: the note written plus a minor third lower. It's an interesting way of expanding the harmonic palette of the mandolin, without adding technical difficulties, and its use is not limited to one musical style.

Since the tremolo is indicated throughout, the staccato dot is used to indicate a note without tremolo. The split-string chord in measure 4 is both editorial and optional (see Part I, chapter 6). You might try a split-string trill on the second course in measures 89 and 90 (see chapter 6).

Understanding the style of interpretation—music that's *not* on the page, but only implied by context—is essential. Multi-string tremolo and compound-picking patterns can help to bring out the most from this elegant period piece.

Queen of Beauty
Waltz

William Moyer, 1920
Ed. August Watters

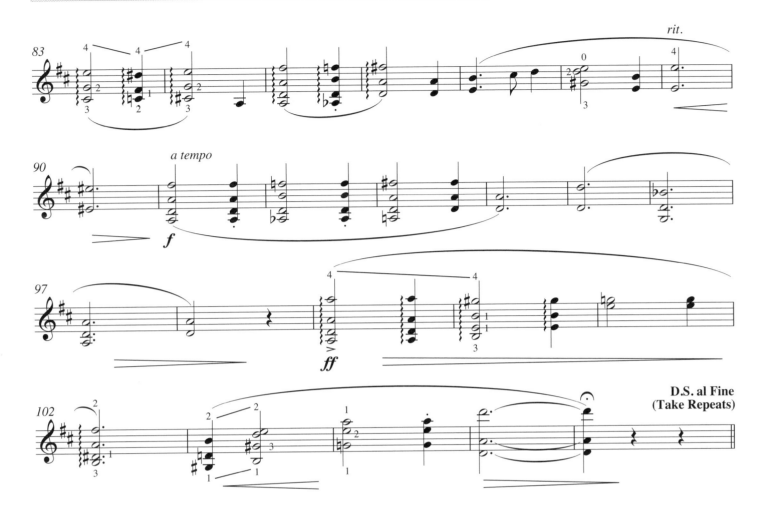

MOZART, "DEH, VIENI ALLA FINESTRA"

Mozart's "Deh, Vieni alla Finestra" ("O, Come to the Window!") from *Don Giovanni* is one of the most famous classical mandolin melodies. The image of the mandolin serenade outside a young maiden's window has deep roots in European art and culture, and would certainly have been familiar to Mozart's audience.

Deh, Vieni alla Finestra
from *Don Giovanni*

Wolfgang A. Mozart
Ed. August Watters

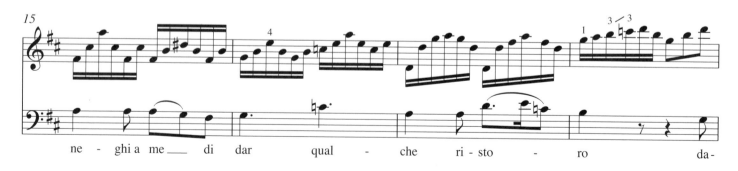

van - ti a gli - oc -chi tuoi   mo - rir___ vo - gli - o.

Tu ch hai   la boc - ca dol - ce   piu_____ che il

mie - le,   tu che il zuc - che - ro por - ti in   mez - zo il cuo -

re,   non es - ser gio - ia

mia,   con   me cru - de - le!   Las - cia -ti al - men _ ve -

der,   mio   bell'____ a - mo - re!

BEETHOVEN, "ADAGIO"

This "Adagio" is one of several concert works composed by Beethoven for mandolin with keyboard accompaniment. Although we might take pride that Beethoven evidently took our instrument seriously as a chamber music instrument, we must also consider that these works reportedly resulted from Beethoven's infatuation with a young lady who played mandolin! Although I have arranged the keyboard part for mandolin and mandocello, the original mandolin part here has not been altered.

Adagio

Ludwig van Beethoven
WoO 43b
Ed. August Watters

Adagio

Ludwig van Beethoven
WoO 43b
Ed. August Watters

CALACE, "MOTO PERPETUO"

"Perpetual motion" is a form that explores instrumental technique via a running stream of notes. Raffaele Calace's "Moto Perpetuo" is also an interesting concert piece, with a variety of moods and textures. I have edited this version slightly, omitting a few measures of extreme high-register playing that indicate Calace's skill in that area was virtually beyond reach, by today's standards.

Moto Perpetuo

Raffaele Calace
Op. 124
Ed. August Watters

CALACE, "SILVIA"

"Silvia" is one of Raffaele Calace's last solo compositions, and also one of his easiest. Calace uses none of his usual sweeping right-hand pyrotechnics, instead building this piece on a straightforward duo-style approach, popular song form, and Golden Era-style harmonization. When you have mastered the works in this book by Calace, Munier, Denis, and Leone, you will be ready to move on to Calace's *Preludes.* These masterpieces of the Virtuoso Era still set the technical standard today for the virtuoso classical mandolinist.

Silvia
Gavotte

Raffaele Calace
Op. 187
Ed. August Watters

Form: AABBACCAcoda

+ = left-hand pizzicato

MUNIER, "2ND ARIA VARIATA"

The "2nd Aria Variata" of Carlo Munier is a solo concert piece in a romantic style. Munier introduces left-hand pizzicato (beat 2 in measures 9 through 12), and emphasizes alternate picking throughout, except when D-U-D-U-D-U triplet picking applies.

2nd Aria Variata

Carlo Munier
Ed. August Watters

MUÑOZ, "L'AMI"

Juan Carlos Muñoz (b. 1964) is a mandolinist/teacher/composer within the German edua-
tional system who brings a uniquely pan-European perspective to teaching and composing
for mandolin. His short work "L'ami" explores unusual textures combining open strings with
high-register notes.

L'ami

from *Estampes*, GVH KM-2053

Juan Carlos Muñoz
Ed. August Watters

CRATON, "JANNEMAN EN ALEMOER"

Composer John Craton dedicated movements of his *Variations from Der Fluyten Lust-hof of Jakob van Eyck* to individual members of Holland's Het Consort, under the direction of Alex Timmerman. The variations combine a medieval sense of modality with a post-Romantic approach to mandolin composition.

Janneman en Alemoer
from *Variations from Der Fluyten Lust-hof of Jakob van Eyck*
for Niels Godart

John Craton
Ed. August Watters

ABT, "THE BROOKLET"

One of my personal favorites, "The Brooklet" by Valentine Abt represents the best of the Golden Era. It combines a technical style based in eighteenth- and nineteenth-century classical mandolin with emerging, turn-of-the-century popular musical styles and a sophisticated way of building variations. The result should be inspirational for today's mandolinist seeking to understand the roots of the American mandolin, and the relevance of those roots today.

The Brooklet

Valentine Abt
Ed. August Watters

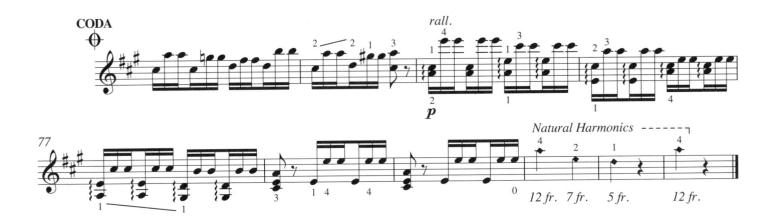

MORRIS, "DREAM ON"

"Dream On" is a Golden Era solo built on standard ragtime-style chord progressions. This type of work was often published at the turn of the twentieth century in general-interest mandolin-guitar magazines, suggesting that jazz-style chord vocabulary, and the skill to read it, was commonly understood by mandolinists of that era.

Dream On

J. Robert Morris
Op. 11, No. 2, 1904
Ed. August Watters

NAKANO, "STUDIO III"

Jiro Nakano was one of the most unique and influential voices in the growth of classical mandolin in late twentieth-century Japan. As a composer he developed an intricate style that advanced mastery of left-hand technique in particular. "Studio III" features hauntingly beautiful textures and an elegant economy of motion. Maestro Nakano's work as a teacher, composer, conductor, and collector of mandolin music did much to advance the state of modern classical mandolin worldwide.

Studio III

Jiro Nakano
Op. 23-3
Ed. August Watters

DELLA LANCIA, "SCHERZO"

Giuseppe della Lancia (also known as Giuseppe Milanese) contributed some brilliant compositions with a sophisticated harmonic vocabulary and an advanced chord-melody concept. His "Scherzo" is worth careful study. Tremolo should be reserved for notes with an accent (>).

Scherzo

Giuseppe della Lancia
Ed. August Watters

WATTERS, "THE REVENGE OF SAINT PATRICK'S SNAKES"

This is what happens when you start composing early in the morning, the day after Saint Patrick's Day! If you are playing this solo, you will probably need to shorten some of the durations in the lower voice. The fingerings are intended for playing solo, both staves at once, using split-string technique. Alternatively, if you approach this piece with two mandolins playing duet, you may find better fingerings for each part individually.

The Revenge of Saint Patrick's Snakes
Solo Split-String Study, or Duet for Two Mandolins

August Watters

WATTERS, "PRELUDE NO. 1"

Like *Tillamook Impressions* (figure 6.16), "Prelude No. 1" combines all the various techniques—both historical and new—presented in this book. I hope you will find it to be a challenging and rewarding concert piece.

Prelude No. 1

August Watters

WATTERS, "JUST THE FOUR OF US"

"Just the Four of Us" is not so different from the duo-style study "Just the Two of Us" (figure 6.4). "Just the Four of Us," however, adds another dimension: split strings. I recommend mastering "Just the Two of Us" first. It's a good way to learn any split-string study, learn it first without the split strings. In this book, any split-string study can be played without the split-string double-stops by omitting the lower of the two notes.

Just the Four of Us
Split-String Duo-Style Study

August Watters

PART III
Classical Arrangements for Solo Mandolin

Part III presents arrangements of classical compositions originally conceived for other instruments. Some of the works here are literal transcriptions; others are heavily adapted or arranged for mandolin. The Camidge "Gavotte" and the Krieger "Minuet" include play-along accompaniment tracks with parts for mandolin, guitar, and/or mandola.

CAMIDGE, "GAVOTTE"

Many classical concert works are based on folk dance forms. This "Gavotte" was composed for organ, but adapts well to mandolin. Adapting other literature to mandolin ensemble is a rewarding and creative process, although it requires great sensitivity to style and context.

**Audio
14, 15, 16**

Gavotte
from *Six Concertos for Organ* Op. 13

Matthew Camidge
Arr. Andrew Boden
Ed. August Watters

ABEL, "ALLEGRO"

This "Allegro" by Carl Abel was composed for viola da gamba, a fretted relative of the modern cello. I prefer the rich sonority of the GDAE mandola (octave mandolin) for this piece, but it works well on mandolin too. On long phrases with wide intervals (such as measure 10), I use an all-downstrokes approach to unify the tone of the two distinct lines. The fingerings here are for mandolin. On mandola, I use more open strings than indicated.

Allegro
from *27 Pieces for Bass Viol*

Carl Abel
WKO 186
Ed. August Watters

BACH, "PRELUDE"

This "Prelude" is perhaps the best known work from Bach's *Cello Suite No. 1*, an extended work that contains many beautiful pieces. This edition has been transposed up a fifth (from the original key of G major) to match mandolin tuning, but I especially like to explore Bach's cello suites in their original keys using the CGDA mandola. If you can read treble clef intervallically, it's not too difficult to also read bass clef!

Prelude
from *Cello Suite No. 1*

J.S. Bach
BWV1007
Ed. August Watters

GOUNOD, "SERENATA"

This serenade originated as a Victor Hugo poem set to music by Charles Gounod. Carlo Munier's audiences would have been familiar with this Romantic melody, so this must have been a crowd pleaser—much as we might arrange popular songs today to reach a general audience. Today's audiences are less likely to remember Gounod's lovely melody, but Munier's arrangement remains a charming solo piece. You may wish to add a few chords to support the melody (such as I have done in measures 30–34), or just rely on tremolo to carry the long notes.

Serenata

Charles Gounod
Arr. Carlo Munier
Ed. August Watters

KRIEGER, "MINUET"

This arrangement of Johann Krieger's "Minuet" highlights the similarities between Baroque music and jazz, such as fluid, improvised accompaniments outlining chord progressions featuring "cycle 5" motion. The accompaniment language of Baroque music, figured bass, is not so different from our modern chord symbols. Figured bass is normally realized by continuo (any group of accompaniment instruments). Although this language predates the modern mandolin, there is also a history of plucked string instruments, such as theorbo and Baroque guitar, participating in the continuo. When Baroque music is played by modern instruments, mandolin is an excellent choice!

Minuet

Johann Krieger
Arr. August Watters

**Audio
17, 18, 19**

TELEMANN, "LARGO"

G.P. Telemann's music often explores melody more than the nuances of any particular instrument—fortunately for us, since much of his music translates well to mandolin. This "Largo" is a literal transcription of the notes Telemann wrote for solo violin, but I have added phrasing marks where notes on different courses of the mandolin can easily be sustained together.

Largo
from *12 Fantasias for Violin without Bass*

Georg Philipp Telemann
TWV40
Ed. August Watters

TELEMANN, "ALLEGRO"

Telemann's "Allegro" from *12 Fantasias for Flute* makes an excellent chord-melody study. Although the melody was originally for flute alone, this arrangement adds mandolinistic chord voicings to complete the implied harmonies.

Allegro
from *12 Fantasias for Flute*

Georg Philipp Telemann
TWV40
Arr. August Watters

BACH, "SARABANDE"

The exquisite solo violin music of J.S. Bach is a natural fit for mandolin. Although Bach intended vertical chord voicings to be rolled across the violin fingerboard, most can be sounded simultaneously on the mandolin's frets. Still, it's best not to be too literal when interpreting Bach's chord voicings. An occasional revoicing for the sake of playability is sometimes necessary when reinterpreting Bach's violin music for mandolin.

Sarabande
from *Partita No. 2 for Violin*

Johann S. Bach
BWV 1004
Ed. by August Watters

MUNIER, "BARCAROLLE"

The barcarolle is a form based on a 6/8 rhythm meant to capture the sound of a gondolier's pole propelling its passengers through the canals of Venice. This "Barcarolle" by Munier originated as a melodic study, to which I have added chord voicings to complete the harmonies. As you work through this piece, keep the accent on beats 1 and 4 of the 6/8 measure, with activity on the third and sixth beats, so the rhythm sounds like "ta-TA (rest) ta-TA (rest)" corresponding to beats "6–1 (rest) 3–4 (rest)."

Barcarolle

Carlo Munier
Op. 216, No. 6
Arr. August Watters

BEETHOVEN, "ODE TO JOY"
Version 1

Version 1 of Beethoven's "Ode to Joy" from his ninth symphony uses (mostly) familiar mandolin voicings, so if you've mastered the chord voicing materials in chapter 5, version 1 will soon be within reach. Version 2 retains more of Beethoven's original harmonizations.

Ode to Joy
Version 1

Ludwig van Beethoven
Arr. August Watters

Version 2

Ode to Joy
Version 2

Ludwig van Beethoven
Arr. August Watters

BRACKETT, "SIMPLE GIFTS"

Originally composed by Shaker Elder Joseph Brackett, "Simple Gifts" is best known through
Aaron Copland's settings, which have worked their way deeply into popular consciousness.
I often use this piece to connect to listeners, who always like to hear a familiar tune. There's
humor as the variations develop, and they gradually realize that nothing stays simple forever!

Simple Gifts

Joseph Brackett
Arr. August Watters

FOSTER, "OLD FOLKS AT HOME"

I grew up thinking of this tune as an American folk song, but "Old Folks at Home" belongs to an earlier generation of popular music in antebellum America. Printed arrangements were the main product of the music industry, and arrangements for mandolin and mandolin ensembles became very common as their popularity grew, late in the nineteenth century. Today, players in the folk and roots music scenes often think of reading music as a recent intrusion into the folk process, but the popularity of written music during the Golden Era suggests that music reading skills were much more developed then than today. Here is my own modern version of this Stephen Foster favorite.

Old Folks at Home

Stephen Foster
Arr. August Watters

PUCCINI, "O, MIO BABBINO CARO"

Puccini's aria from *Gianni Schicchi* is, for me, the height of romanticism in Italian opera. I haven't attempted to indicate dynamics and tempo changes because these details, and the emotional content of this music, can be fully captured only through careful listening. In addition to tremolo technique, the compound-picking patterns in Part I, chapter 5 are useful to create swells from multiple stops, accentuating the beauty and the drama of the romantic style.

"O, mio babbino caro"
from *Gianni Schicchi*

Giacomo Puccini
Arr. August Watters

DVOŘÁK, "HUMORESQUE"

Dvořák's "Humoresque" uses primarily the three-note chord voicings from figures 5.2 and 5.4. The connecting sixteenth notes require careful preparation of the left hand, since there is so little time before the following chord is sounded. The problem is usually solved by playing the sixteenth note using a finger not involved in the following chord. The melody begins in the highest voice of the three-note chord, and switches to the lowest voice in measure 9. Like the other well-known melodies earlier in this section, it's important to learn by listening to different versions for stylistic and interpretive ideas. Much of the humor in this piece lies in the way you play with the audience's expectations, so feel free to reinterpret the dotted eighth-sixteenth rhythm to keep them guessing.

Humoresque

Antonin Dvořák
Arr. August Watters

BIBLIOGRAPHY

Bickford, Zarh Myron. *The Bickford Mandolin Method, Vol. 1.* New York: Carl Fischer, 1920.

Branzoli, Giuseppe. *Theoretical and Practical Method for the Mandolin.* Boston: Oliver Ditson Company, 1892.

Calace, Raffaele. *Metodo per Mandolino.* Naples: 1892.

Cottin, Jules. *Célèbre Méthode Complète Théoretique et Pratique de Mandoline.* Paris: Alphonse Leduc, 1912.

Cristofaro, Ferdinando de. *Méthode de Mandoline.* Paris: Henry Lemoine, 1892.

Denis, Pietro. *Méthode pour apprendre à jouer de la mandoline sans maître.* Paris: 1768.

Fouchetti, Giovanni. *Méthode pour apprendre facilement á jouer de la mandoline á 4 et á 6 cordes.* Paris: c. 1771.

Köhler, Ernesto. *Mandolinenschule für den Selbstunterricht geeignet.* Leipzig: Jul. Heinr. Zimmerman, 1892.

Krempl, Josef. *Mandolinen-Schule.* Leipzig: Universal-Edition, 1897.

Leone, Gabriele. *Méthode raisonnée pour passer du violon à la mandoline et de l'archet a la plume.* Paris: n.d. (18th century).

Mair, Marilynn. *The Complete Mandolinist.* Pacific, MO: Mel Bay, 2007.

Munier, Carlo. *Scuola del Mandolino.* Florence: Adolfo Lapini, 1891.

Odell, Herbert Forrest. *Odell Method for the Mandolin.* Boston: Oliver Ditson Co., 1906.

Pettine, Giuseppe. *Pettine's Modern Mandolin School.* Providence: Rhode Island Music Co., 1930.

Pietrapertosa, Jean. *Methode de Mandoline.* Paris: Schott, 1892.

Schick, Otto. *Mandolinen-Schule.* Leipzig: C.F. Peters, 1890.

Sparks, Paul. *The Classical Mandolin.* Oxford: Oxford University Press, 2005.

Tyler, James, and Paul Sparks, *The Early Mandolin.* Oxford: Oxford University Press, 1992.

Vorpahl, Reinhold. *Neue Reform-Schule für die Neapolitanisch- oder-Römische.* Berlin: A. Köster, 1902.

ABOUT THE AUTHOR

August Watters is a multi-stylistic, improvising mandolinist, composer/arranger, and teacher who has performed with some of the leading figures in today's revival of this elegant instrument, including Carlo Aonzo, Don Stiernberg, Marilynn Mair, and Butch Baldassari. His work as an interpreter, improviser, composer, and arranger bridges contemporary classical music, jazz, folk music traditions, and the historical concert mandolin repertoire.

Watters is also deeply involved, as a composer/arranger and performer, in the advancement of music for mandolin-guitar ensembles. He is the founder of the New England Mandolin Ensemble, Boston Mandolins, the Festival of Mandolin Chamber Music, and Cape Cod Mandolin Camp. He also maintains an active schedule of performances in solo and duo formats.

Photo by Robert Patton

As an international clinician and soloist, Watters has performed in Italy, Germany, England, the Czech Republic, Canada, and the United States. He is also an Emmy® Award-winning arranger, with dozens of studio credits as arranger, orchestrator, and conductor for television and film music. Watters holds a Masters of Music Education from Boston University and a Bachelor's of Music from Berklee College of Music (summa cum laude), majoring in jazz composition and arranging.

Watters is a professor of ear training at Berklee College of Music, where he has been recognized by the String Department and the college administration for developing and teaching new curricula designed for the needs of improvising string players. His New Acoustic Music Ensemble has trained successive generations of roots-oriented improvisers since its inception in 2000. In addition, Watters has taught Berklee classes in harmony, composition, arranging, and interpretation, as well as private mandolin lessons. August Watters' mandolin, model "Lucia," was built in 2010 by Carlo Mazzaccara. His mandola (in GDAE tuning) was custom-designed and built for him in 2004 by Rozawood Instruments.